Savage Snows

Walt Unsworth

Savage Snows

The Story of Mont Blanc

Hodder & Stoughton

LONDON SYDNEY AUCKLAND TORONTO

British Library Cataloguing in Publication Data
Unsworth, Walt
    Savage snows: the story of Mont Blanc.
    1. Mountaineering——Blanc, Mont (France
    and Italy)——History   2. Blanc, Mont
    (France and Italy)——History
    I. Title
    796.5'22'094449   GV199.44.M65

    ISBN 0 340 39777 2

Hodder and Stoughton Editorial Office: 47 Bedford Square, London WC1B 3DP.

Contents

Illustrations

PICTURE CREDITS

1 Andrew Harper   4 J. M. Patchett   7 Brian Evans
2 John Cleare   5 Rob Collister   8 French National Tourist Office
3 C. R. Rowson   6 Steve Ashton   9 Walt Unsworth

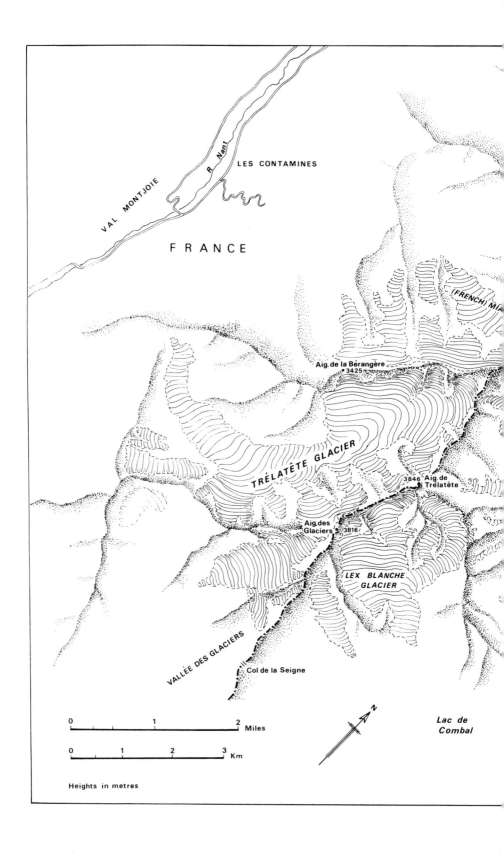

VAL MONTJOIE

R. Nant

LES CONTAMINES

FRANCE

(FRENCH) MI...

Aig. de la Bérangère
• 3425 m

TRÉLATÊTE GLACIER

3846 Aig. de
Trélatête

Aig. des
Glaciers • 3816

LEX BLANCHE
GLACIER

VALLÉE DES GLACIERS

Col de la Seigne

0   1   2 Miles

0   1   2   3 Km

Heights in metres

Lac de
Combal

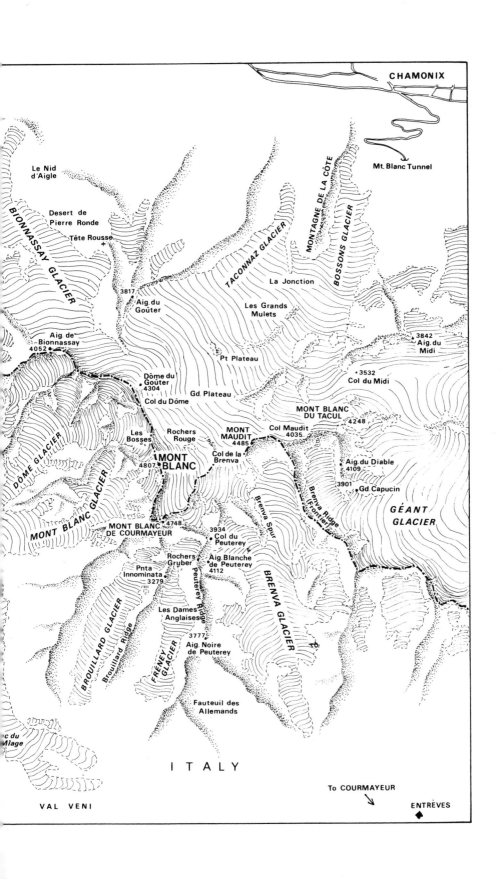

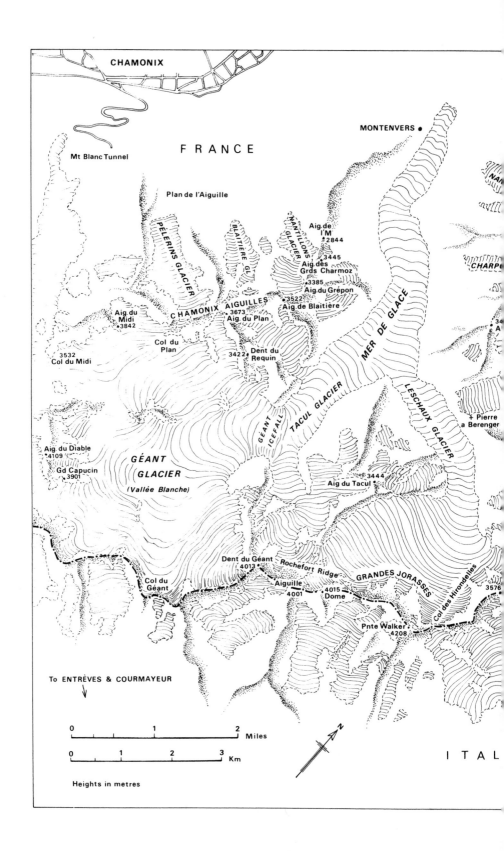

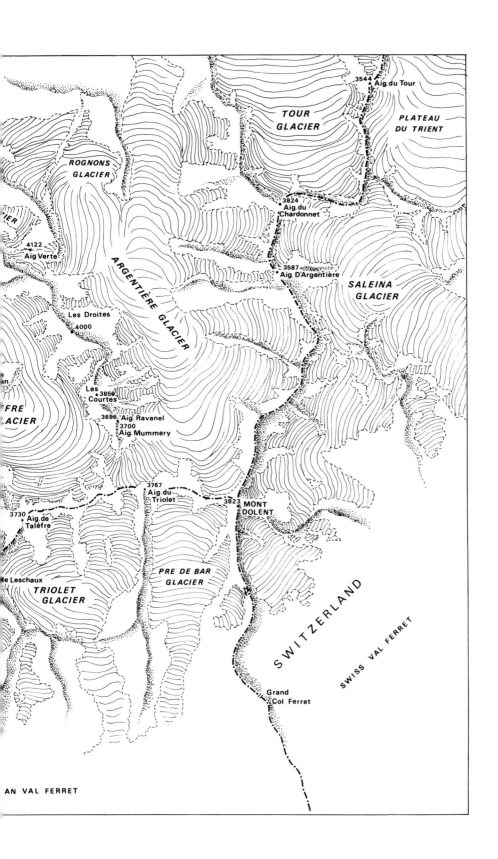

TOUR
GLACIER

PLATEAU
DU TRIENT

3544
Aig. du Tour

ROGNONS
GLACIER

3824
Aig. du
Chardonnet

4122
Aig Verte

ARGENTIÈRE GLACIER

3587
Aig. D'Argentière

SALEINA
GLACIER

Les Droites
4000

FRE
ACIER

Les
Courtes

3856

3696 Aig. Ravanel
3700
Aig. Mummery

3767
Aig. du
Triolet

3823 MONT
DOLENT

3730
Aig. de
Talèfre

PRE DE BAR
GLACIER

le Leschaux

TRIOLET
GLACIER

SWITZERLAND

SWISS VAL FERRET

Grand
Col Ferret

AN VAL FERRET

Introduction: Alps on Alps

The highest mountains in Western Europe lie stretched like a necklace around the top of Italy, separating that country from its neighbours. In the west they rise near Nice on the Mediterranean and curve east for some five hundred miles to end on the outskirts of Vienna. For the most part they are covered in permanent snow and ice which over the centuries has worn away the underlying rock to give the peaks their present shapes. Glaciers flow down between the peaks towards the surrounding valleys – rivers of ice moving imperceptibly but relentlessly, grinding and plucking at the rock, and refuelled by fresh snowfalls each winter: the process is never-ending.

In earlier times the peasants who lived amongst these mountains regarded the snowy heights and the glaciers as evil places best left alone. To their simple minds the distant rumble of an avalanche could easily be equated with the roar of a dragon stirring in its icy lair high amongst the great peaks. Those who were brave enough to investigate sometimes never came back; swallowed by the dragons more than likely, or at least swallowed by the treacherous crevasses of the glaciers – what difference if the end result was the same? Even those who didn't believe in dragons, and there weren't many, were agreed that the snowfields and glaciers were of use to neither man nor beast.

So it is hardly surprising that when strangers first came to the mountains and asked what they were called the locals thought they were enquiring about the upper pastures where the cows were driven in summer. These were called *alps* and so the mountains too became the Alps.

The Alps are separated by nature into recognisable groups and sixty miles south-east of Geneva Mont Blanc and its satellites form one such group, limited to the west by the Col du Bonhomme and to the east by the Col Ferret, a distance of some twenty miles. On its northern edge the group is defined by the deep rich valley of the Arve in which lies Chamonix, the principal village of the Mont Blanc area. To the south the narrow rocky valleys of the Veni and Ferret cut off the mountains in a line as straight as a ruler and where they meet, to form the Aosta Valley, is the charming Italian village of Courmayeur. Between Chamonix and Courmayeur the distance is only about ten miles, and since there are dozens of peaks to fit into this 200 square miles of wilderness, the effect is one of compression, with the mountains seemingly locked together in close embrace, squeezing out their glaciers like toothpaste from a tube.

Until the building of the Mont Blanc road tunnel in 1962 there was no easy way through these mountains. Crossing from north to south meant high and icy cols, some of which were difficult even for trained mountaineers and all of which were to some degree dangerous. Carriage roads were out of the question and even that lifeline of mountain districts, the mule track, was impossible. Yet communication between the seven valleys which surround these mountains was politically desirable because until 1860 the whole area, with the exception of the extreme eastern end which was in Switzerland, belonged to the House of Savoy. Even after that date, when the northern part was ceded to France (a move confirmed by popular plebiscite) and the southern part integrated into the newly founded Kingdom of Italy, it was still necessary for commercial and cultural exchanges to take place. Fortunately, in an area as compact as this it was not difficult to link together various mule tracks around the mountains' periphery. These had to cross high cols like the Ferret (2531m) and the Seigne (2516m) which ruled out vehicular traffic, but at least they were free of permanent snow and ice. Using these tracks it was possible to reach Courmayeur from Chamonix in three days although, according to one nineteenth-century guidebook writer, 'a good walker could do it in two'.

This was the foundation of the Tour du Mont Blanc, a popular walk which completely encircles the massif in about ten days. It is usually walked in an anti-clockwise direction starting from the Chamonix valley and it leads from France into Italy, then to Switzerland and finally back into France, visiting en route the seven valleys of Mont Blanc. If we follow it in our imagination it will give us some idea of the positions of the different parts of the group.

From the valley of the Arve it crosses the Col de Voza into the Val Montjoie, which is the western end of the range. This was the way some of the early explorers came when they were trying to climb Mont Blanc, because the great Bionnassay Glacier, which has its origins on the mountain, sweeps down to this valley. Other important peaks at this end are the Aiguille de Trélatête and Aiguille de Bionnassay. The Tour then crosses some high cols to the Val des Glaciers; a wild, lonely place but one which belies its name since it probably has less in the way of glaciers than the other valleys.

From the head of the Val des Glaciers the way then goes over the Italian frontier at the Col de la Seigne into the narrow, dramatic Val Veni on the southern edge of the mountains. A chaos of glaciers comes crashing down into the valley – the Miage, Brouillard, Frêney and Brenva – which drain the savage southern face of Mont Blanc. Towering over the valley is the formidable looking Aiguille Noire de Peuterey.

At the end of the Val Veni, where it joins the Val d'Aosta, is the compact village of Courmayeur, a counterpart to Chamonix though far less developed economically because, until the coming of the Mont Blanc Tunnel, Courmayeur was very isolated. Now it echoes to the rumble of juggernauts on the way from Northern Europe to Milan or Turin.

From Courmayeur the Tour du Mont Blanc continues along the southern edge of the range by means of the narrow, rocky Val Ferret. Over the valley, though not seen to advantage, hangs the Rochefort Ridge with peaks like the Géant and Grandes Jorasses, the Aiguille de Triolet and Mont Dolent. The frontier between Italy and France has followed the crest of these peaks from Mont Blanc through to Mont Dolent, where it meets the Swiss frontier and so all three nations share this mountain, which is the south-east cornerstone of the group.

From the Italian Val Ferret the path leads over a col of the same name into the Swiss Val Ferret, which forms the eastern limit. The big mountains are curiously reticent here, standing well back, sheltered from view by minor peaks and it isn't until the Trient valley is reached that something of the old majesty is recaptured with the splendid Trient Glacier. This is the last of the seven valleys – across the easy Col de Balme lies the village of le Tour and the vale of Chamonix.

Chamonix-Mont Blanc (to give it its full title which nobody ever uses) lies in the middle reaches of the upper Arve valley, the largest of several villages strung out along the river. Ribbon development has done much to rob most of the other villages of their individuality, though le Tour and Argentière at the top end of the valley and les Houches at the bottom end still retain something of their own character. But Chamonix overpowers the rest; full of its own importance as the avowed world centre of mountaineering and an international ski resort. It is a bustling, busy, lively place which has been called the Blackpool of the Alps, though this is unfair on both places. Despite the modern buildings, the tourist-thronged streets, Chamonix still retains a whiff of the propriety which Kiss-Me-Quick Blackpool long ago abandoned.

A small railway runs along the valley connecting the villages with each other and the outside world and from Chamonix station another railway, of the rack-and-pinion kind, clanks its way up through the forests to Montenvers, a hotel complex perched on the edge of the Mer de Glace, the largest glacier of the Mont Blanc range. Several cable-cars swing up from the valley to the surrounding heights, including one to the summit of the Aiguille du Midi, from where it is possible to continue the journey high over the Vallée Blanche and down to Entrèves near Courmayeur.

Chamonix grew originally round an eleventh-century priory which ruled the valley, often harshly, until 1786 when the commune bought its freedom – particularly ill-timed, for had they waited three years for the French Revolution, they could have had it for nothing! The priory itself was burned down in 1758.

The name of Chamonix had been adopted for the village in 1330 and it appeared in Mercator's Atlas of 1595 so it was obviously well known even before the first trickle of tourists began in the early eighteenth century. The mountains themselves were known simply as les Glacières and the highest summit, so readily seen from the village, was called Mont Maudit – except by the villagers themselves. With immense good sense they had always called it by its most obvious name – Mont Blanc, the White Mountain – for it rises high and wide and white like no other peak in the vicinity. By the late eighteenth century the

16

name had been universally adopted and that of Mont Maudit transferred to an adjacent peak.

One of the reasons Chamonix became known to the outside world before most other Alpine centres was because Mont Blanc could be seen from Geneva; the distant snows seeming to drift above the clouds. It was known to be the highest mountain in the Alps and to have the most spectacular glaciers, so though the journey lasted an arduous three days, some of the more adventurous travellers included it in their itinerary. What they saw when they got there exceeded all imagination: the great white mountain itself rising high above the village, with a circle of attendant peaks, some of them large and snow covered, others smaller, rocky and spiky like Gothic spires. The large Bossons Glacier poured down from Mont Blanc, right to the valley floor where blocks of ice as large as houses, broken from the glacier, rested incongruously amongst the grass and trees. The walk up to Montenvers – usually known as 'the Mountain' in those early days – soon became a popular excursion, revealing fresh wonders like the huge placid ice stream of the Mer de Glace wending its way through the heart of the region, and the dramatic obelisk of the Petit Dru.

The English were there early and long before Windham and Pococke made it popular a lovelorn swain had written to a lady describing the scenery: 'Here, Madame, I see five mountains which are just like you . . . five mountains, Madame, which are pure ice from top to bottom.'

Her reply is not recorded.

1 'With you I fear nothing'

The ancient city of Geneva lies in a little enclave of Switzerland tucked on to the western end of Lac Leman. Only a narrow strip of territory on the northern shore of the lake connects it with Lausanne and the rest of Switzerland; otherwise it is entirely surrounded by France.

In the eighteenth century it was very different. In those days Geneva was an independent city-state, still surrounded by its medieval walls, where the drawbridges were pulled up each evening and where no visitor could obtain a night's lodging without a permit from the Captain of the Guard. The city was ruled by a patrician class of staunch Calvinists whose ordinances were so strict that it was even forbidden to walk the streets on Sunday during church services.

Yet despite such seemingly austere conditions, Geneva was at this time much more liberal than most of Europe and so became a natural haven for political refugees, scholars and social outcasts – there was a flourishing colony of young Englishmen, for example, some of whom had come to finish their schooling and others who had been banished to the Continent by their exasperated fathers for misdeeds at home.

It was the visit of two Englishmen from Geneva in 1741 which brought Chamonix into greater prominence. William Windham was an athletic young man known in fashionable London circles as 'Boxing Windham' because of his pugilistic abilities. He came from Fellbrigg in Norfolk but spent much of his time on the Continent because he and his father didn't see eye to eye. He was about twenty-three at this time and had just met Richard Pococke, fourteen years his senior and already a noted traveller in the Middle East. The idea of a visit to 'les Glacières' was Windham's. 'I had long had a great desire to make this excursion,' he says, 'but the difficulty of getting company made me defer it.' Pococke was just the man with whom to add action to words. An inveterate traveller, he eventually visited many of the most remote corners of Britain and, according to one authority, if he had published his travels earlier instead of leaving them until late in life, he would have had much of the credit that eventually went to Thomas Pennant. He later became a somewhat fiery Protestant Bishop in Ireland.

Together with six companions and five servants, 'all of us well armed', they left Geneva on June 19 and arrived at Chamonix three days later after a very rough journey during which their horses lost shoes on several occasions. When eventually they arrived at their goal they asked to be shown 'les Glacières' and the natives pointed out the ice streams which flowed down into the valley – presumably the Bossons Glacier and Mer de Glace. The Englishmen were not content with this however – 'We thought we had come too far to be content with so small a matter' – and resolutely set out to climb 'the Mountain', which was Montenvers, guided by villagers who thought them quite mad but were being well paid for their trouble. The natives pointed out that only crystal seekers and chamois hunters ventured into the mountains, and they sometimes did not return.

They found the climb to Montenvers steep and laborious, taking four and three-quarter hours over a walk which can today be done in half that time. In a letter to a friend Windham described for the first time the nature of the Chamonix Aiguilles – 'the tops of which being naked and craggy rocks, shoot up immensely high; something resembling old Gothic buildings or ruines . . .'

But it was the ice which attracted the Englishmen most. They scrambled down onto the Mer de Glace, examined the crevasses and celebrated by drinking the health of Admiral Vernon and a success to British arms – no doubt much to the astonishment of their guides. Not that these good wishes from on high did Vernon much good, for he was struck off the Flag List four years later.

The party returned to Chamonix by sunset, where the villagers were not only glad to see them safely back but surprised that the expedition had been so successful.

In his letter Windham wrote a detailed account of their journey. This was circulated around the Geneva establishment and in the following year a party from that city, led by an engineer named Peter Martell, repeated the journey for the purpose of making various scientific measurements, as Windham had suggested. This was in tune with the age: science was becoming a new God whose influence was to spread throughout the mountain world for almost the next hundred years. By the botanists and mineralogists Nature could be observed and collected; by the physicists it could be measured – not that the early scientists thought of restricting themselves to one discipline, for in a world where everything was new, there were none of the scientific demarcations we have today. The behaviour of glaciers came under intense scrutiny and was, for a century, to be a constant source of controversy. The effect of altitude on air pressure and temperature was also of interest and was the reason given for making many of the early ascents; no self-respecting mountaineer would attempt anything new without taking along a barometer and thermometer. These delicate instruments were frequently broken and sometimes, one feels, the climbers were rather glad of it. As time went on, science became more of an excuse than a reason for climbing mountains; it lent an air of respectability to what might otherwise be seen as irresponsible adventures by people who should know better.

Martell published an account of his journey which also included Windham's original letter. Its wide circulation ensured the popularity of Chamonix and 'les Glacières' so that by 1779 Dr John Moore (father of the more famous son who was to die at Corunna) complained: 'One could hardly mention anything curious or singular without being told by some of those travellers, with an air of cool contempt – "Dear sir, that is pretty well; but, take my word for it, it is nothing to the glaciers of Savoy." '

Moore, incidentally, visited the region with the Duke of Hamilton who, not content with Montenvers, thought he might get a better view if he climbed the Aiguille du Dru. He was stopped in this startling enterprise by 'a part of the rock which was perfectly impracticable'. He was a century before his time.

Intellectually Geneva was a powerhouse, birthplace of Rousseau, adopted home of Voltaire, and there were scientists, too – for this was the Age of Reason – amongst whom was Horace Bénédict de Saussure, Professor of Natural Philosophy at the Geneva Academy, a post he had attained at the age of twenty-two.

De Saussure was one of those to whom the gods gave everything, brains, wit, good looks and a happy marriage. But he also had a second love – the Alps.

From the limestone crags of the Salève above the city, de Saussure must have seen the magnificent distant panorama of 'les Glacières' many times as a boy. The vision haunted him and he wrote to tell a friend how much he longed to see the mountains at close quarters, nor was he disappointed when, in 1760 at the age of twenty, he made his first journey to the Chamonix valley. He fell in love with the place at once, explored the foothills and set foot on some of the glaciers with all the enthusiasm of an excited schoolboy. It was, one feels, the sheer mystery and magic of the mountains which enthralled him and also roused the scientific urge of discovery. Virtually nothing was known about the world of rock and ice which confronted de Saussure at Chamonix.

It was fairly obvious that Mont Blanc was the highest mountain, though nobody had ever stood on its summit (or any of the other summits for that matter). Perhaps to the eager young man from Geneva the summit didn't seem too inaccessible, yet he was shrewd enough to realise that none of the local peasants would waste time and energy trying to climb it without good reason. So he offered a cash prize – 'a rather considerable sum,' he called it – as an inducement to anyone who would make the first ascent and promised to meet the expenses of those who tried and failed. There was not exactly a rush to take him up. A villager called Pierre Simond attempted the mountain in a half-hearted fashion but he got nowhere and it was many years before anyone tried again. During this time the scientist had extended his own knowledge of the Alps which in the years ahead he was to present in a series of volumes, *Voyages dans les Alpes*.

Some of his scientific contemporaries from Geneva were becoming more adventurous. In 1770 the de Luc brothers climbed a mountain called the Buet (3099m). It was the first peak of such height to be climbed in the Mont Blanc region, and only the fourth in the Alps, the others being Rochemelon, Mont Thabor and Titlis. The de Lucs were quite astonished at the way they were unaffected by the altitude: 'they were forced by the absence of any disagreeable sensation to remark what a wonderful adaptive machine is the human body, whose equilibrium remains undisturbed within while the atmosphere without is so changed in density.' Of course, we now know that man can even reach the summit of Everest without oxygen equipment, but it has taken two centuries to acquire this knowledge – the de Lucs' ascent of the Buet was the first step on the road.

Nevertheless, de Saussure's reward for the first ascent of Mont Blanc might have been quietly forgotten had not Marc Théodore Bourrit arrived on the scene. He was a failed painter of miniatures whose plausibility and contacts were such that he had been appointed Precentor of Geneva Cathedral, a sinecure which enabled him to indulge his interests in mountains and writing. He was mountaineering's first great publicist – 'the indefatigable Bourrit' someone once called him. He was not a scientist like the de Lucs or de Saussure, though he followed the fashion in such matters. He might have been called a gentleman-amateur, except that neither of these terms could be applied to Bourrit. He was egocentric, womanising and extremely jealous of anyone who might do something better than he could himself. He was certainly jealous of the de Luc brothers and de Saussure, though he was wise enough not to say so in public since these men were important members of the Geneva establishment. De Saussure, always a man of easy going nature, put up with Bourrit's idiosyncracies: the de Luc brothers hated him.

Despite all this his books found a wide acceptance throughout Europe and in the tight-knit society of late eighteenth-century Geneva, Bourrit was something of a literary lion. People were genuinely flattered to meet him; including on one occasion a young medical student called Michel-Gabriel Paccard, whom he was later to meet again in very different circumstances.

Bourrit first came to Chamonix in 1766 and at once saw the commercial advantages that an ascent of Mont Blanc would bring to Chamonix and himself. He embarked on a propaganda campaign to try and rouse public opinion, cleverly seizing on de Saussure's offer of a reward, to give the enterprise both respectability and excitement.

There is no suggestion that Bourrit wanted de Saussure's reward for himself, or that he wished to take part in the first ascent. Later on, his attitude to actually climbing the mountain changed, but his main aim throughout was to promote the conquest of Mont Blanc and to write the bestselling account of it.

He did not have much success at first. It was not until 1775 that the first real attempt was made. In the July of that year four Chamonix men – Michel and François Paccard, Victor Tissay and Jean-Nicholas Couteran, son of the Chamonix inn keeper, slept at the foot of the Montagne de la Côte and next day scrambled up the rocks and onto the ice at la Jonction. From there they pressed on up the glacier to an area known as the Petit Plateau. Tissay and Couteran investigated the rocks of the Grands Mulets, but then mists began to swirl around the mountain and the four young men, frightened by the increasingly hostile environment, made a hurried retreat to the village.

Two months later there arrived at Chamonix Thomas Blaikie, a self-taught Scottish landscape gardener and botanist who had been sent to the Alps by wealthy English patrons to collect plant specimens. In Geneva he was introduced to de Saussure and other members of the scientific community who advised him to go to Chamonix, where he was bound to find the sort of plants he was seeking. They gave him a letter of introduction to the Royal Notary of the district, a man of some importance, called Joseph Paccard. In his diary Blaikie (never a good speller) wrote of his arrival in the village:

> After refreshing at a publick house at Chamouni went with my letter I had for Mr Paccard, found him at home; he seems to be a man of respect in this place, he has three sons very genteel young men after some descourss there was two of them proposed to go along with me in purpose to conduct me and at the same time learn plants; the oldest is learning surgery the second is a Priest and the youngest about 20 is studying at the university of Turin to be a Doctor.

In fact, the youngest was eighteen and his name was Michel-Gabriel Paccard. He was destined to play a seminal role in the conquest of Mont Blanc.

He was the same young man who had been introduced to Bourrit. Whether he had been impressed by Bourrit's writings or inspired by the recent attempt on Mont Blanc (the two Paccards in that attempt were his cousins) there is no way of knowing, but he was fascinated with the mountain and kept detailed records of all the attempts and ascents until 1825 – except, ironically, the one which concerned him most.

After a day spent on the Mer de Glace with two of the Paccard sons, Blaikie embarked on a remarkable mountain exploration with young Michel-Gabriel. The two young men – Blaikie was only twenty-five – climbed up through the woods above the village towards the Chamonix Aiguilles until they reached the stony hollow of the Plan de l'Aiguille, where today there is a cable car station. A little way above this they came to a tiny lake, the Lac du Plan de l'Aiguille, from where they traversed below the spiky summits of the aiguilles, crossing on the way the Blaitière and Nantillons Glaciers. Their precise itinerary is not known, but it does seem to have been the first tentative exploration of the pinnacles which dominate Chamonix. Presumably they were botanising as they went along; at any event the journey took them all day and they spent the night at the chalets of Blaitière-Dessus, below the Nantillons Glacier. (This rude shelter was still comfortable when I spent a night there in the 1960s.)

Next day they climbed up towards the aiguilles again and traversed below them to the Bossons Glacier. They crossed this to the head of the Montagne de la Côte then, climbing the Taconnaz Glacier, reached the Aiguille du Goûter: 'exceeding high perpendicular rocks which towards the mountain supports this bed of snow and ice which forms Mont Blanc and these Glacières'. This was far enough. They returned to Chamonix, happily sliding down the ice whenever they could, using their iron-tipped alpenstocks to support them.

After a night's rest they climbed the Brévent, which was already becoming a celebrated viewpoint, then two days later visited the Jardin de Talèfre, a wild glacier region overshadowed by a ring of icy peaks: the Verte, Triolet, Talèfre, Droites and Courtes amongst them. This was the very heart of the Mont Blanc massif, a place previously known only to the most daring crystal seekers.

In the course of a week this adventurous pair had accomplished the first serious exploration of the Mont Blanc group ever attempted, perhaps even the most serious mountain exploration anywhere. Did Paccard have an ulterior motive?

Was he already probing the defences of Mont Blanc with the thought of making an ascent?

For the next eight years, little was attempted on Mont Blanc. In 1779 an unknown Frenchman had made a meagre try, then in 1783 three villagers had a go. They got no further than their predecessors, though this did not prevent one of them, Lombard Meunier, from boastfully proferring advice to those who would follow: 'It is of no use to take any provisions for the journey; all that is wanted is an umbrella and a scent bottle.'

Meanwhile, Bourrit had begun to wonder whether anyone would ever make a serious attempt on the mountain and was slowly reaching the conclusion that he should do the job himself. The more he thought about this the more it appealed to him, for there would undoubtedly be much to be gained in the way of fame and distinction. It would need to be done properly, however, with due scientific gravity; a mere scramble for the summit might be good enough for peasants seeking a reward but would certainly not do for Marc Théodore Bourrit.

There were two practical difficulties. First, he was not a scientist and possessed no scientific instruments (de Saussure refused to lend him his) and secondly, he hated the cold and discomfort involved in mountain climbing. It is true he had climbed the Brévent and the Buet several times, but his love for mountains, genuine enough though it was, was an abstract thing divorced from the harsh reality.

The second of these problems he pushed to the back of his mind, but the first was something he had to tackle if his expedition was to have credibility. He had to have a scientist as a partner. He didn't want de Saussure because de Saussure was too famous; any success would be attributed to him and that was not part of Bourrit's game plan. He asked a scientist called Gosse, but Gosse turned him down and he knew it would be a waste of time asking the de Lucs. Then he remembered Michel-Gabriel Paccard.

By this time Paccard was the village doctor in Chamonix. He had had a good education in Turin and Paris, was interested in science and was a corresponding member of the Turin Academy. He was intelligent, cultured and athletic. He was also somewhat short tempered, touchy, and not a man to suffer fools gladly. Nevertheless, he was probably flattered by Bourrit's approach and so he agreed to join the venture, recruiting two local men to act as guides.

The expedition took place in September 1783. They climbed up the long crest of the Montagne de la Côte and slept the night at the top of the rocks. Next day, however, the weather was bad and Bourrit, thoroughly frightened by the savage surroundings in which he found himself, refused to go any further. 'M. Bourrit did not dare go on the ice,' wrote Paccard in his diary. It was not an accidental choice of words; it embodied the disgust which the doctor felt at his fallen idol's cowardice.

Given Paccard's forthright nature it is unlikely that he kept his feelings hidden during the descent to Chamonix. It must have been an embarrassing time for both of them, but for Paccard this unhappy excursion might well have been the root cause of much future sadness, because Bourrit was not the man to forget or forgive a slight.

Both men now had ambitions on the summit. In the following year Paccard explored the Géant Glacier but found no route from it to the summit. He next turned his attention to the western side of the mountain, where the great Bionnassay Glacier curls down towards the Val Montjoie. With a few hardy companions he climbed up the flanks of the glacier and scrambled up rocks to reach a place known as the Tête Rousse, where some stones poked out of a small glacier. Above them rose the broken rock ribs of the Aiguille du Goûter. Paccard noted in his diary that there was dangerous stonefall on this face of the Goûter – there still is, 200 years later, though this is now the most popular way of climbing Mont Blanc. On this occasion, however, Paccard went no further than the Tête Rousse. With his companions he returned to Chamonix, having broken two barometers during the course of the expedition.

Convinced that his new route was an important step forward, Paccard wrote describing it to de Saussure. Bourrit also got to hear of it and on September 16, only a week after Paccard's attempt, he set off with five guides to climb it. They all reached the Tête Rousse next morning but Bourrit felt ill so after making a sketch of the vale of Chamonix he retreated to the stony wastes of the Desert de Pierre Ronde, accompanied by three of the men, and gradually back to the chalets at the foot of the Bionnassay Glacier, where he fell asleep.

Meanwhile the two remaining guides, Marie Couttet and François Cuidet, pushed on from the Tête Rousse up the broken central rib of the Aiguille du Goûter to its snowy summit. Above them lay the higher Dôme du Goûter, a simple snow mountain shaped like an upturned pudding basin, which they crossed to find themselves at a broad col beyond which was an outcrop of rock, where the Vallot Hut now stands. From these rocks they could see a snow ridge, humped like a camel's back, rising to the top of Mont Blanc. How tantalisingly close it seemed! And yet les Bosses du Dromadaire were unknown and must have seemed formidable. By now the day was well advanced so the two men returned to Bourrit to tell him of their adventures.

It had been a very brave effort. Couttet and Cuidet had gone higher on the mountain than any of their predecessors. The way to the summit seemed open.

The following summer, 1785, was wet and cold. No attempt could be made on the mountain until September when Couttet, this time accompanied by Lombard Meunier, again reached the foot of the Bosses Ridge but they were driven back by storms.

De Saussure himself now decided to take a hand. Bourrit had told him of the guides' success, which confirmed what he had already heard from Paccard about the suitability of the Bionnassay route. He felt obliged to Bourrit for keeping him informed and though he would probably have preferred to make an attempt accompanied only by guides, felt compelled to invite Bourrit to accompany him. Bourrit responded by bringing along his son Isaac as well, a bumptious youth of twenty-one.

It had been de Saussure's plan to camp as high as possible on the mountain before making the summit assault, but Bourrit changed all that. Remembering his two previous attempts and the discomfort involved in a night out on the mountain, Bourrit insisted on having a stone cabin built at the Tête Rousse to serve as a base. To this were carried palliasses, sheets, blankets, pillows, wood and provisions, as well as de Saussure's scientific instruments. Fourteen men were needed for this, nine of whom remained behind to help with the climb.

Next morning they commenced the ascent of the Goûter rocks. It must have been a strange sight as they struggled upwards, Couttet leading the way. Paccard, who recorded all these attempts in his diary, wrote:

M. Bourrit was held by the collar of his coat by Tournier, and was leaning on the shoulder of Gervais. In the difficult places a barrier was made by a bâton, on which M. de Saussure was able to lean, both going up and descending. Young M. Bourrit, almost ill, ascended by holding to Cuidet's coat.

The going must have been very slow for at eleven o'clock they were still on the Goûter rocks when de Saussure called a halt and asked two of the guides to go ahead and reconnoitre. When they returned, after about an hour, it was with the news that there was much fresh snow up above which would make the climb laborious, possibly dangerous. In such a poor season this was only to be expected. De Saussure, who hated soft snow, immediately decided to go no further. Everyone was glad of this except young Bourrit who wished to continue but was over-ruled. De Saussure then conducted some experiments before they all descended to the hut.

The Bourrits continued their descent to Bionnassay but de Saussure spent another night at the hut in order to make further scientific observations. Once back in Geneva both the Bourrits wrote to de Saussure criticising his climbing ability, especially on the descent, when the scientist had had the good sense to be roped to two guides. The younger Bourrit, who had obviously inherited all of his father's less admirable traits, wrote:

Sir, do you not envy me my twenty-one years? Who will wonder if a youth of this age, who has nothing to lose, is bolder than a father of a family, a man of forty-six?

To which the scientist replied:

A moderate amount of boastfulness is no great crime at your age . . . you descended agilely enough on the easy places, but in the difficult places you were, like your father, leaning on the shoulder of the guide in front and held up behind by another . . . In no language in the world can that style of progress be termed agile climbing.

The discovery of the Bionnassay route, meanwhile, was beginning to cause some consternation in Chamonix. To reach this from the village meant a tedious climb over the Col de Voza and the Chamoniards were astute enough to realise that in order to avoid this the logical starting point was St Gervais, not Chamonix. If Mont Blanc *was* climbed by the Bionnassay route it wouldn't take the tourists long to realise the same thing and they would flock to St Gervais, leaving Chamonix out in the unprofitable cold.

Consequently, in the season following de Saussure's vain attempt, 1786, a group of the most active men in the village decided to hold a race to see which was the quickest way of reaching the Dôme du Goûter. They were convinced it could be reached direct from Chamonix without the need for the long detour round by Bionnassay, but nobody had ever been that way so there was no telling what hidden difficulties there might be. A trial was the only answer: two men were to sleep at the Desert de Pierre Ronde above the Bionnassay Glacier whilst three others slept at the top of the Montagne de la Côte, above Chamonix. Then, on the following day, both groups were to make their way to the rendezvous. Whoever got there first must obviously have been following the easier route.

So on the evening of June 7, Pierre Balmat and Marie Couttet slept at the Pierre Ronde whilst Joseph Carrier, Jean-Michel Tournier and François Paccard (the doctor's cousin), slept on top of the Montagne de la Côte. As Carrier and his companions were just about to settle down for the night they were unexpectedly joined by a fourth man, a crystal hunter also called Balmat, but no relation to Pierre. Jacques Balmat lived in the valley at the hamlet of Pélerins.

Balmat's appearance was not welcomed. He was twenty-four years old (older than any of the others), reputed for his cunning and generally disliked. On the other hand, he had as much right to be on the mountain as anyone else, so the others reluctantly agreed that he could join them, provided he had his own food and could take care of himself.

Early next morning, aided by firm, crisp snow, the four men made their way across the crevasses of la Jonction to the Grands Mulets rocks, then struck up the snow towards Mont Blanc. The way opened before them without difficulty: a bit steeper in some parts than others, perhaps; one or two awkward crevasses, but nothing to stop their progress. Before long they reached the wide snow bowl of the Grand Plateau from where they plodded up an easy slope to the Dôme du Goûter. To their immense delight they were first to the rendezvous, beating the others by one and a half hours and so demonstrating the superiority of Chamonix as a starting point.

Having proved their point, they then crossed the Col du Dôme and examined the Bosses Ridge leading to the summit of Mont Blanc. What they found appalled them: the ridge was steeper than they imagined and fell away sheer on either hand to dizzying depths. Too afraid to proceed, the Chamonix champions turned for home, convinced that this was not the way to climb Mont Blanc.

Meanwhile, Jacques Balmat remained behind, looking for crystals amongst the Vallot rocks. When eventually he started to descend the others were already far ahead. By this time the sun had softened the snow, making the going very arduous and Balmat, desperately tired, fell further and further behind. The others, true to their word, left him to look after himself. When night fell, he was still on the glacier.

By now he was too tired to care where he was. When he came to a particularly large crevasse which the others had jumped across he couldn't summon the necessary energy, so he slumped down in the snow and fell into a troubled sleep. When he awoke next morning he was shivering with cold and his clothes were rimed with hoar frost – but he was surprised to find himself very much alive, for it was firmly believed in those days that to sleep out at high altitude meant certain death. Without more ado he made his way down to Chamonix.

Some time later Balmat was to give a slightly different version of this story, tailored to suit the events which followed. According to him, when he awoke on that morning he went back up the glacier to the Grand Plateau to explore it further and there discovered an entirely new way of climbing Mont Blanc, which eliminated the dreaded Bosses Ridge. Later still, he claimed that he spent a further four days in exploration. But neither of these tales was true, for he was back in Chamonix by eight o'clock that morning, consulting Dr Paccard about his sun-blistered face.

Events were now moving towards their bizarre climax. Paccard had been studying the mountain for three years; talking with the men who had taken part in various attempts and scanning the peak through his telescope until he knew every detail by heart. His favoured route – the Bosses Ridge – had been found impracticable and the other ridge leading down left of the summit looked even worse because it was interrupted by a big cliff – Paccard was not to know that this was an optical illusion. It seemed to him that the only chance lay in tackling the mountain face on. In his diary he wrote:

> Marie Couttet, who had examined these slopes from the Dôme du Goûter, thought them hopeless. It seemed to me that one might be able to climb them by a broad bank of snow that slopes steeply up to the left . . . I determined to make another attempt. My own guide was away and so when Jacques Balmat offered his services I accepted his offer and engaged him as a porter.

But why Balmat, of all people? Was it because the crystal hunter had proved he could survive a night in the open, and Paccard thought he might have to do so again? Years later, when telling his story to Alexandre Dumas, Balmat had a different version:

> I went to Paccard and said, 'Well, Doctor, are you determined? Are you afraid of the cold or the snow or the precipices? Speak out like a man.' 'With you I fear nothing,' was his reply.

On the evening of August 7, 1786, Dr Paccard and Jacques Balmat bivouacked at some rocks near the top of the Montagne de la Côte at the place now known as the Gîte à Balmat. From there at four next morning they began their ascent. Route finding was difficult because the season had been warm and much of the snow was gone off the glacier, leaving a complex maze of crevasses between which the two men wove their way. Even when they did find a snow bridge, it could not be relied upon, as Paccard later described:

> Four times the snow bridges, by which we tried to cross the crevasses, gave way beneath our feet, and we saw the abyss below us. But we escaped catastrophe by throwing ourselves

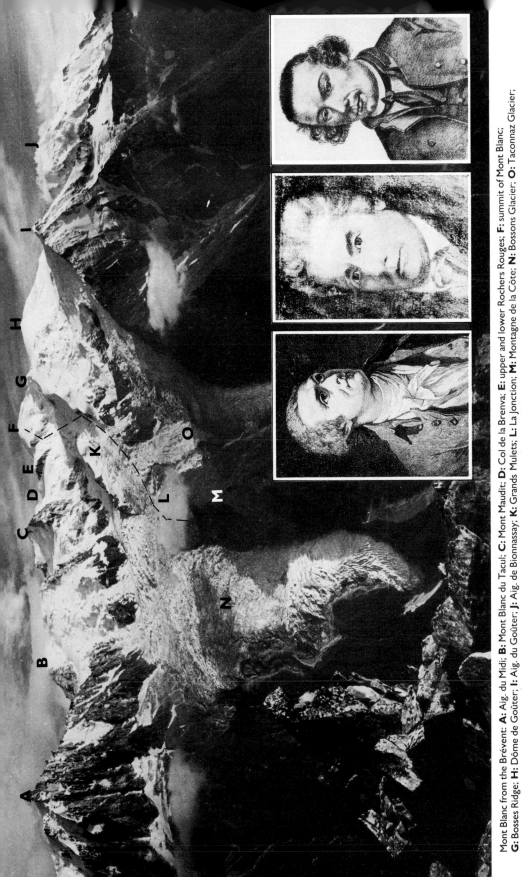

Mont Blanc from the Brévent. **A:** Aig. du Midi; **B:** Mont Blanc du Tacul; **C:** Mont Maudit; **D:** Col de la Brenva; **E:** upper and lower Rochers Rouges; **F:** summit of Mont Blanc; **G:** Bosses Ridge; **H:** Dôme de Goûter; **I:** Aig. de Bionnassay; **J:** Aig. du Goûter; **K:** Grands Mulets; **L:** La Jonction; **M:** Montagne de la Côte; **N:** Bossons Glacier; **O:** Taconnaz Glacier; dashed line shows route of first ascent.   *Inset l to r:* H.B. de Saussure, Michel-Gabriel Paccard, Jacques Balmat.

The Brenva Face of Mont Blanc. The skyline is the upper Peuterey Ridge above the steep Grand Pilier d'Angle. The ice arête of the Old Brenva stands out clearly centre picture.

A climber on the famous arête of the Old Brenva under conditions more favourable than on the first ascent by Moore's party.

flat on our bâtons laid horizontally on the snow, and then, placing our two bâtons side by side, we slid along them until we were across the crevasse.

It took eight hours to pass the Grands Mulets rocks.

Beyond the rocks there was fresh snow, deep, soft and fatiguing. The glare from the sun burnt into their eyeballs. Balmat wanted to give up. He was suddenly filled with remorse at leaving his wife to care for a sickly new-born infant and he felt that he should return to be by her side. Paccard would have none of it, recognising this as mere excuse on Balmat's part. It is true, the child was mortally ill – but Balmat had known that when he set out. The doctor relieved Balmat of some of his load and they shared the arduous task of breaking the trail through the deep, soft snow.

As the afternoon wore on the two men laboured up the slopes above the Grand Plateau, following the ramp between the upper and lower Rochers Rouges. This they found to be steeper than anything they had so far encountered, with little ice walls barring their way from time to time. Higher up it became very exposed: a nervy business where Paccard picked out steps with the iron spike of his bâton in the trickiest places. Each man stepped up warily – they were not roped together. Paccard felt sure that they would have to endure a high bivouac, but there did not seem to be any resting place.

They struggled on, halting to catch their breath every few paces, though now the heat of the day was past and the bitter cold ate into their marrow, preventing them from resting long. Once they were above the Rochers Rouges, Paccard made straight for the top but Balmat, still carrying the heavier load, took an easier slope and had to put on a spurt to catch up with his companion. They reached the summit together, watched by two black birds. It was 6.23pm, August 8, 1786.

The first thing they did was to tie a kerchief on one of their bâtons and stick it in the summit snow. Most of Chamonix was watching through spy-glasses and saw the signal clearly, including two friends of de Saussure who left immediately for Geneva to break the good news. Then Paccard set about his scientific experiments, which lasted about thirty minutes. At 6.58pm – ten minutes before sunset – they began their descent, plunging down the upper slopes in an almost reckless fashion in a hopeless race against the oncoming night. Fortunately, it was a night of clear sky with a bright moon which enabled them to see almost as well as during the day. A little before midnight they reached their bivouac place at the Montagne de la Côte.

It had taken them some fourteen and a half hours to climb Mont Blanc and five hours to descend; a quite remarkable tour de force. Now they were utterly exhausted, their hands were frostbitten and their eyes smarted from snowblindness, especially Paccard, who was almost totally sightless. They bivouacked until dawn, then made a slow return to Chamonix, Balmat leading the blind doctor down the Montagne de la Côte.

And so the race was won by two outsiders, for no betting man who had been watching the game thus far would have placed any money on Balmat and Paccard. De Saussure, Bourrit and a group of prominent guides had been making the recent running, so how come these two had met with success so swiftly, and whose idea was it anyway? These were the questions uppermost in the minds of everyone concerned – questions which were to sour relationships between Paccard and Balmat and lead to a great injustice.

Balmat hurried off to Geneva to collect the reward, which was augmented by a German admirer and by the King of Sardinia. He talked to de Saussure and he talked to Bourrit. Paccard stayed quietly at home, talking to no one.

De Saussure then went to Chamonix, intent on making another ascent, but the weather was bad so he called on the doctor, questioning him closely over the details of his epic climb. He persuaded Paccard that he should write an account for publication and this the doctor promised to do. On his return to Geneva, de Saussure talked to his friends about the book and even issued a prospectus to ensure it would have a ready sale.

This was altogether too much for Marc Théodore Bourrit. Consumed with jealousy over Paccard's success (and perhaps remembering the way the doctor had once cold shouldered him) he wrote and published *Letter on the first journey to the summit of Mont Blanc*, in which he declared that the hero was Balmat and that Paccard was nothing more than a craven fool who had to be dragged most of the way up the mountain. He tried to get de Saussure's approval before publication, but the scientist was so horrified at what Bourrit had written that he persuaded him to tone it down – but not enough. Because of Bourrit's popularity with a wide reading public, the infamous *Letter* spread across Europe, making Balmat an international hero.

Meanwhile, Paccard's own story was being quietly suppressed. When the doctor completed his manuscript he gave it to J. P. Béranger, scientist and publisher (after whom the Aiguille de la Bérangère is named) in the expectation that it would quickly appear and put a stop to the lies Bourrit was spreading. But Paccard was like an innocent lamb in the lion's den of Geneva intrigue; not everyone was as honest or kindhearted as de Saussure, and certainly not Béranger, who was a close friend and supporter of Bourrit. Béranger prevaricated about the manuscript, repeatedly sending it back for alterations and corrections, until in the end Paccard lost heart. The book was never published and the manuscript disappeared – to become something of a literary *cause célèbre* many years later, as scholars combed Europe in a fruitless quest for 'Dr Paccard's Lost Narrative'.

Because he had written a full account of the climb for publication, Paccard gave only the briefest notes in the little book he had so religiously kept recording all the attempts on the .mountain. He did write in his own defence to local newspapers, but these were not widely read and Bourrit's story went virtually unchallenged. In Chamonix itself the village was divided into Balmat and Paccard factions and on one occasion the two men had a fist fight in the village inn.

As the years went by, Balmat came to believe the story he told Bourrit. Forty-six years after the event when he was interviewed by Dumas, he embellished it some more. Dumas embroidered it further still until it had the same degree of historical accuracy as the story of Alfred and the cakes, or James Watt and the boiling kettle. Nevertheless, this was the story the public accepted: Bourrit and Dumas between them put paid to the Chamonix doctor. Years later the village erected a statue to Balmat. They forgot all about Dr Paccard.

Ironically, it was the search for the 'Lost Narrative' which finally rehabilitated Paccard's reputation, for though the scholars did not find what they were seeking they did come across a lot of other evidence which showed conclusively the part Paccard had played in the first ascent. In the de Saussure archives they came across this character assessment of the doctor: 'This modest and sympathetic character has been very unjustly relegated to the second rank behind the somewhat theatrical figure of his countryman Balmat. Paccard was a mountaineer of great merit.'

And what afterwards became of the four men whose names are inextricably linked with the first ascent of Mont Blanc? Paccard continued as the village doctor and was elected Mayor in 1794. Two years later he married – Marie Balmat. He continued to climb and is even said to have been up Mont Blanc again.

Balmat became a local celebrity. He built himself a new house at les Pélerins and was much in demand as a guide. He climbed Mont Blanc five more times, including an ascent with de Saussure in 1787 and with the first woman to climb the mountain, Maria Paradis, in 1809, but eventually he gave up climbing and became a gold prospector. He died in mysterious circumstances – possibly murdered – whilst looking for gold in the peaks above Sixt in 1834, aged seventy-two years.

De Saussure died, full of honours, in 1799 at the relatively early age of fifty-nine, worn out, it is said, by his strenuous Alpine campaigns.

Marc Théodore Bourrit died in 1819. There may be some justice in the fact that of the four men, he was the only one who never succeeded in climbing Mont Blanc.

2 Old Brenva

The ascent of Mont Blanc in 1786 did not lead to any sudden vogue for mountain climbing. Though there were some people for whom mountains held a perpetual fascination – Ramond de Carbonnière in the Pyrenees, or Father Placidus in Eastern Switzerland, for example – mountain ascents tended to be one-off affairs. There was, for instance, the Abbé Murith, who had actually climbed the imposing Mont Velan (3734m) seven years before Paccard and Balmat made their ascent of Mont Blanc, but climbed nothing else – 'too much trouble', he told de Saussure. Velan was Murith's local peak, so to speak, and with few exceptions, Alpine climbs over the next several decades tended to be by local people on a local peak – usually the highest in the neighbourhood – 'because it was there'.

Mont Blanc was different. Because it was the highest mountain in Western Europe, it attracted a wider clientele. In 1787 Colonel Mark Beaufoy became the first Englishman to climb it (fourth ascent) and in 1802 Baron Dorthesen made the first German ascent (sixth ascent). In 1818 a romantic young Pole, Count Antoni Malczewski climbed Mont Blanc (twelfth ascent) and also made the first ascent of the Aiguille du Midi – the first of the Chamonix aiguilles to be climbed. A year later, 1819, came the first American ascent by William Howard and Jeremiah van Rensselaer (thirteenth ascent).

There were, of course, attempts which failed – Bourrit made three such – but it is rather surprising that there should have been any attempts at all as France slid into the turmoil of the Revolution and Europe became engulfed by Napoleon's conquests. Even after Waterloo, when the wars were ended, bands of renegades and deserters made travel in the remoter Alpine valleys hazardous. Yet throughout this troubled period attempts continued to be made on Mont Blanc, some more successful than others.

Two of these are of particular interest because each in its own way marked a stage of the mountain's development.

In mid-July 1809 Jacques Balmat decided to take his two sons, Ferdinand and Jean-Gédéon (aged fourteen), up the mountain. They were accompanied by the guides Michel and Victor Tairraz and Pierre-Marie Frasserand. Just as they were on the point of starting they were astonished at being joined by two local women, Euphrosine Ducroz and Maria Paradis, who asked to accompany them. The liberating spirit of the Revolution had obviously reached the women of Chamonix. For Mme Ducroz the guides had a ready refusal. She was a married woman with responsibilities and they were not prepared to risk her life on Mont Blanc. But for Maria Paradis they had no excuses. Maria was unmarried, a strong serving wench of twenty-eight with a determined character.

Balmat took her by the hand and asked her whether she had really made up her mind to climb the mountain. She assured him she had. 'I am an old wolf of the mountains,' said Balmat, 'and even I will not promise to succeed. All I ask of you is to be courageous.' Maria clapped her hands in joy.

That evening they reached the rocks of the Grands Mulets without difficulty, but next day, July 14, Maria found the going very arduous. The men climbed too quickly for her and by the time they reached the Grand Plateau she fell to the snow utterly exhausted. The guides took her by the arms half pushing, half carrying her as far as the Rochers Rouges where she felt so ill she begged them to drop her in a crevasse and continue the ascent alone. Not surprisingly, they declined to do this, and insisted that she should continue to the top, where, she later said, she was unable to speak or breathe. It was the ninth ascent of Mont Blanc and the first real mountaineering ascent by a woman anywhere in the world.

When Maria returned to Chamonix next day all the women of the village came to greet her and ask her what it was like to climb Mont Blanc, but she refused to tell them anything. 'If you want to know what it is like,' she said, 'go and find out for yourselves.' In later years she opened a little café at Pélerins where she was known as Maria of Mont Blanc and where, thirty years later, she was able to greet Henriette d'Angeville, the second woman to climb the mountain.

The attempt by Dr Joseph Hamel's party in 1820 is notable for a less happy reason: it suffered the first fatalities on Mont Blanc in the thirty-four years since Paccard and Balmat had climbed the mountain. Fourteen parties had reached the summit by then and dozens more had attempted it, all without mishap and, indeed, after the 'affaire Hamel' there wasn't another death on the mountain for forty-four more years. Say what you will about the competence of the party, one can't help feeling that Dr Hamel was just plain unlucky.

Dr Hamel was a Russian savant and Counsellor of State to the Czar. His motive for climbing Mont Blanc was scientific and to this end he had borrowed apparatus from de Saussure and others and was accompanied by a technician from Geneva, a M. Selligue. After failing on a new route from St Gervais via the still unclimbed Bosses Ridge, he adjusted his sights to the ordinary route from Chamonix. On August 18, accompanied by Selligue and two Oxford undergraduates, Joseph Dornford and Gilbert Henderson, together with twelve guides, he made his way up to the Grands Mulets where the party encamped for the night. A violent storm swept over the camp that evening and next day, the weather still being uncertain, they decided to remain at the Grands Mulets. Two guides were sent down to Chamonix for fresh provisions.

By the morning of the 20th, M. Selligue had had enough: '. . . a married man had a sacred and imperious call to prudence and caution where his own life seemed at stake'. Two of the guides accompanied him down whilst the rest of the party, now eleven strong, began the ascent. They reached the Grand Plateau without incident, where Hamel actually paused to write out two notes announcing his arrival at the summit, leaving blank spaces to insert the hour.

So far the party had been roped together in threes but as they came to tackle the steep slopes leading up to the Rochers Rouges they decided to unrope. The use of the rope was improperly understood in those early days and young Dornford later explained their decision: 'All such plans as that of fastening themselves together with a rope would be utterly useless, besides the insupportable fatigue which this method of proceeding would occasion.'

As they approached the Rochers Rouges, Dr Hamel suddenly felt the snow give way beneath his feet. He jabbed his alpenstock into the slope, but without effect. The next instant he found himself engulfed in a maelstrom of snow, which carried him downwards, suffocating, crushing. When at last he managed to raise his head above the snow he found the whole party were being swept down the slope towards a huge crevasse. For almost 400 metres the slide continued. The avalanche poured into the crevasse, filling it to the brim; then it stopped with a sudden, awful silence.

The survivors, shell-shocked, looked around them: three of their number were missing, buried beyond recall in the crevasse. All were guides: Pierre Balmat, Pierre Carrier and Auguste Tairraz. Hamel and Dornford made a forlorn attempt to scrape away the snow in the crevasse in the hope of finding the missing men, but it was quite useless.

Forty-one years later the guide Ambroise Simond was strolling near the foot of the Bossons Glacier when he noticed some human remains poking out of the ice. During the next four years other relics appeared. It is six miles from the crevasse below the Rochers Rouges to the foot of the Bossons Glacier, but the ice moves inexorably downwards. Mont Blanc was giving up her dead.

In the sixty-seven years between 1786 and 1853 there were forty-five ascents of Mont Blanc, an average of two every three years. Then quite suddenly, in 1854, there were sixteen ascents in that one year, most of them British. Quite obviously such an enormous increase can't be attributed to chance: something must have occurred which stimulated British interest in Mont Blanc. What occurred was Albert Smith.

Albert Richard Smith was the son of a surgeon in Chertsey, a profession in which he followed his father, studying in London and Paris. At the age of nine he had read an account of the Hamel accident in a children's book called *The Peasants of Chamouni* and so intrigued was he by the story that throughout his boyhood he read every book on Mont Blanc he could lay his hands on. Such was his obsession that he even constructed a small moving panorama showing details of the ascent and using this as a background he would vividly recount the Hamel story to his terrified little sister, who was press-ganged for the occasion. Though Smith probably didn't realise it at the time, he had hit upon a way to fame and fortune.

In the autumn of 1838, during a break in his studies in Paris, he was able to fulfil his cherished ambition of visiting Chamonix to gaze at Mont Blanc. His only hope of actually climbing the mountain, since he was a penniless student, was to attach himself to some other party as a porter, but in this he was out of luck. He visited the Mer de Glace, however, then spent the rest of his vacation in Italy. When at last he returned home to Chertsey to practise medicine, he amused local literary societies by giving vivid talks about his travels, illustrated once more by an ingenious moving panoramic backcloth. In 1841 he moved to London, initially as a surgeon, but a growing reputation for light literary pieces – he was an original contributor to *Punch* – induced him to give up medicine and earn his living by the pen. He turned out sketches, plays, novels and pantomimes with apparent ease and considerable success. His great strength lay in knowing exactly what the public wanted and how to provide it.

The money he made from his writings enabled him to visit Constantinople and Egypt in 1849. On his return he wrote a book about it, but he also decided to turn it into a public entertainment called *The Overland Mail*, which was simply a more professional version of the moving panorama idea with which he had once amused his sister and Chertsey society. It proved immensely popular.

Meanwhile, Smith had not forgotten his first love, Mont Blanc. He had visited Chamonix several times over the years but when *The Overland Mail* closed in August 1851, Smith determined to climb Mont Blanc.

At Chamonix he met up with three Oxford undergraduates, the Hon. W. E. Sackville West, C. G. Floyd and F. Philips who were themselves about to make an attempt on the mountain and though these young gentlemen were a bit sniffy at first, they readily agreed to join forces with Smith once they discovered he was 'Mr Albert Smith, the well known comic author'.

Albert Smith reached the summit of Mont Blanc on August 13, 1851. The ascent was remarkable only for the number of guides employed – sixteen, plus twenty porters as far as the Grands Mulets – and the quantity of provisions entailed, including ninety-one bottles of wine and three bottles of cognac. Little wonder that the ascent was made in an alcoholic haze and Smith fell fast asleep on reaching the summit! On their return to the valley they formed up in marching order and entered Chamonix in triumph, to the firing of cannons and the cheers of the villagers. Amongst the onlookers were Sir Robert Peel and John Ruskin, who thought the whole affair was thoroughly un-English. Ruskin was later to pen his diatribe against mountain climbing:

> The Alps themselves, which your own poets used to love so reverently, you look upon as soaped poles in a bear-garden, which you set yourselves to climb and slide down again 'with shrieks of delight'. When you are past shrieking, having no human articulate voice to say you are glad with, you fill the quietude of their valleys with gunpowder blasts, and rush home, red with cutaneous eruption of conceit, and voluble with convulsive hiccoughs of self-satisfaction.

Ruskin had Albert Smith very much in mind when he wrote that.

When Smith returned to London he began work on an entertainment called *The Ascent of Mont Blanc* which had its first performance on March 15, 1852 at the Egyptian Hall in Piccadilly and ran without break for almost seven years. In form it was similar to his previous productions – a moving panorama of Alpine scenes, achieved by means of a large translucent roller screen, lit from behind, in front of which Smith told the story of Mont Blanc and his own ascent. Put like that it sounds a rather dull affair, but Smith was anything but dull; he was the Barnum of the lecture hall. The show was interspersed with topical material, patter songs and humorous asides. Pretty girls dressed in Alpine costume decorated the stage and great St Bernard dogs, complete with brandy flasks, lolled in front of the stalls. It was a prodigious hit, had three Royal Command Performances and made Smith a very rich man. As Edward Whymper later remarked, had Smith not died at an early age, the show might be running yet.

Thousands of people saw the show, found it amusing, and let it go at that. But, and this was important for mountaineering, it also inspired quite a few young men and women to take up an Alpine career of their own. 'Smith was the revolutionary who made climbing fun,' said one historian, and he was right. Within a few years the Alpine Club, the world's first mountaineering club, was formed in London and from that date mountaineering never looked back.

In the sixty-nine years between the first ascent and 1855 nobody had succeeded in climbing Mont Blanc by any other route than that of Paccard and Balmat, which became known as the *Ancien Passage*. True, this had been improved as to detail and there was an important variation known as the Corridor Route which turns the Rochers Rouges entirely to complete the ascent by the steep slopes of the Mur de la Côte. In 1855, however, J. H. Ramsay with three guides made his way over the Col du Géant from Courmayeur, slept at the foot of the Col du Midi then climbed along the high and lengthy snow ridge towards Mont Blanc, avoiding Mont Blanc du Tacul but climbing Mont Maudit (4465m) en route – the first ascent of this mountain. Once beyond Mont Maudit Ramsay's route joined the *Ancien Passage* at the Mur de la Côte. There was nothing to stop him from reaching the summit of Mont Blanc – except his guides, who, one hour from the top, insisted on turning back because time was running out for a safe return.

In all fairness, I think we can allow Ramsay his route, even though he didn't technically complete it; it was the first ascent from Courmayeur, and, incidentally, Ramsay's first visit to the Alps.

A week later another party approached the Col du Midi from Courmayeur. It consisted of E. S. Kennedy, Charles Hudson, Charles Ainslie, E. J. Stevenson, G. C. Joad and the Smyth brothers, Christopher and James Grenville. Except for young Joad – a delicate youth of fifteen, who was a pupil of Hudson's – it was a strong party, most of whom were fresh from a triumphant first ascent of the highest summit of Monte Rosa, second only to Mont Blanc in the Alps. This time they were less fortunate; the weather was poor, they had a miserable night's bivouac and didn't get far along the ridge, though Hudson, one of the strongest climbers of the day, pressed ahead of the others to make a solo first ascent of Mont Blanc du Tacul (4248m).

Having retreated to Courmayeur the party then followed the Tour du Mont Blanc round the mountain to St Gervais, from where they climbed up to the Tête Rousse, inspected the remains of the hut built for de Saussure seventy years earlier, then camped for the night in another hut, built for chamois hunters. Joad and Stevenson then left them but the rest climbed the Aiguille du Goûter and Dôme du Goûter to find themselves at the foot of the Bosses Ridge. A strong wind was blowing and shreds of mist trailed across the ridge in menacing fashion, lending it a formidable air. They agreed that it was feasible, though none was willing to try and they had no guides to whom they could turn for advice. The great prize of the Bosses Ridge lay within their grasp – and they let it go. Instead, they descended to the Grand Plateau and climbed the Corridor route to the summit. Once there they examined the Bosses Ridge from above and again agreed that there was no difficulty, but they declined to descend it.

It is difficult to imagine how such a strong party failed to climb what is now the most popular route up Mont Blanc. Four years later Hudson, accompanied by Joad and G. C. Hodgkinson and led by the great Oberland guide Melchior Anderegg, laid the bogey by ascending from Chamonix to the Col du Dôme and following the Bosses Ridge to the summit, amazed at how easy it all was. Finally in 1871, two top-class climbers, Leslie Stephen and F. F. Tuckett, led by three of the finest guides, Melchior Anderegg, J. J. Bennen and Peter Perren, started from St Gervais and climbed the Aiguille du Goûter, Dôme du Goûter and Bosses Ridge in one continuous expedition: 'thus achieving the undertaking commenced by de Saussure and his companions seventy-six years before.'

Kennedy and Hudson's party of 1855 may have missed the Bosses Ridge, but they did claim the distinctions of making a new route and making the first guideless ascent. Were they right on either count? Their 'route' was simply an amalgamation of previous routes and was long and inelegant. Whether it has ever been repeated is open to question, and certainly nobody in their right mind would want to repeat it today. They did, of course, make a guideless ascent – but neither Paccard nor Balmat were guides at the time of the first ascent, though Balmat became one later.

What is more interesting is the reason why Kennedy and Hudson did not employ guides on Mont Blanc. Guideless climbing wasn't yet the vogue it was later to become, nor were Kennedy and Hudson trying to start a fashion. They had employed guides on Monte Rosa scarcely a week previous and were to do so again. But not Chamonix guides, for by this time Chamonix guides were organised into the worst form of trades union, whose sole object was to cosset the inefficient and rook the traveller.

It had begun back in 1823 when the Sardinian Government, who were then rulers of Savoy, ordered the guides to form a Corporation and set standard tariffs for various excursions. As the century advanced and Chamonix became part of France, the rules were added to and amended, usually to the advantage of the guides and disadvantage of the travellers. In 1852 it was laid down that any man of Chamonix could be a guide provided he had 'personal probity, combined with physical and intellectual aptitude', but the examination to test these qualities was a farce. From time to time a few good men emerged from the ruck, like Michel Croz, who lost his life in the Matterhorn accident of 1865, or François Devouassoud, the schoolmaster-guide whose climbing ranged well beyond the Alps, but the average standard of guiding was low. Even at the end of the century a famous climber wrote: 'It is a melancholy fact that of the three hundred men now on the Chamonix roll, those who could be relied upon in a grave emergency may be counted almost upon the fingers of one hand.'

Apart from high charges, two aspects of the system annoyed the Victorian mountaineers. First, the number of guides to be employed was usually three or four per climber for the ascent of Mont Blanc, plus porters on a ratio of one for one, including the guides. Thus two young travellers attempting the ascent might have eight guides and ten porters, for whom food and drink had to be provided.

Even more annoying was the rigid rota system whereby the next man on the list got the next job, irrespective of whether he was competent or whether the climber preferred someone else. It often meant that a first-rate guide might find himself carrying a lady's parasol on a stroll up to the Col de Balme, whilst some buffoon was struggling to get his clients safely to the summit.

For many years the only escape from this pernicious system was either to climb without guides at all, or to import a guide from another Alpine region, usually the Oberland, which many of the leading climbers did as the century progressed. Such 'off-comers' were not popular in Chamonix, as can be imagined, and were often abused in the taverns by the local men.

Gradually some of the rules were ameliorated but the political authorities were getting fed up with the complaints, especially from the powerful Alpine Club in London, and in 1892 the Société des Guides de Chamonix, despite vigorous protests by its members, was abolished as a government-controlled Corporation. The guides promptly reorganised themselves as a local society, adopting all the old rules. But by then it didn't really matter much; the hey-day of guiding was about to pass as mountaineers became more self-reliant.

The idea of finding different routes up Mont Blanc, as Ramsay, Hudson and Kennedy did, indicated a new spirit abroad in the Alps. At a time when men were exploring the jungles of darkest Africa and the mysterious deserts of Central Asia, others found that there was an almost equally unknown region in the heart of Europe. The scramble for summits began, slowly at first, but with increasing momentum. The British were in the forefront of this movement and soon there were enough of them to form a club, the Alpine club, founded in 1857 and the first such club in the world. Membership was by election (and still is) which in those days meant one had to be both a climber *and* a gentleman; though quite a few members were elected who weren't really either, and some were refused who were both. When the Continental countries came to form their own Alpine Clubs, they cast their nets much wider: virtually anyone could join who could pay a small annual fee. As a result these clubs became large organisations, divided into regional sections. Their income from subscriptions was substantial and they used the money to build simple accommodation, the Alpine huts, in places where climbers had previously to bivouac. The French, Swiss and Italian clubs all built huts in the Mont Blanc range which have been enlarged and replaced over the years as climbing became more popular.

When Hudson attempted the route from the Col du Midi in 1855, he had originally intended trying something quite different. A friend of his, John Birkbeck, had studied the Italian slopes of Mont Blanc from the Col du Géant and from the Mur de la Côte – that is to say, both up and down – and had come to the conclusion that the mountain could be climbed from Courmayeur via the Brenva Glacier. Hudson passed on this knowledge to

Kennedy and they undoubtedly had this expedition in mind when they went to Courmayeur, but the weather wasn't kind and the Brenva Glacier, hugely fractured by massive icefalls, down which avalanches thundered day and night, seemed too daunting a proposition. The idea was abandoned.

Eight years later A. W. Moore was warned off by the outstanding guides Melchior Anderegg and Peter Perren who described the idea of an attempt on the glacier as 'eine miserable Dummheit' (a wretched piece of folly). A year later, however, Moore, guided by Christian Almer, was traversing the mountain by climbing the Bosses Ridge and descending the ordinary route to Chamonix (an extraordinarily arduous non-stop expedition of twenty-one and a half hours) when they took the opportunity (as Birkbeck had done a decade earlier) of looking down the Italian side from the Mur de la Côte to the Brenva Glacier. From where they stood the snow seemed to slope away quite gently for a considerable distance before disappearing more steeply to the glacier far below. Their experienced eyes could detect no intrinsic difficulties and, like Birkbeck, they too came to the conclusion that a route was possible, provided a safe way could be found through the icefalls of the lower Brenva Glacier. What they failed to appreciate was the extent of the mountain beyond their vision; what they saw was a tempting optical illusion.

And so, on July 13, 1865 a strong party of Alpine Club men gathered at Courmayeur to make a determined attempt on Mont Blanc by way of the Brenva Glacier. Moore was there, of course, and Horace Walker, with whom Moore had already made some notable Alpine first ascents that season, including Piz Roseg, Pigne d'Arolla and Ober Gabelhorn in a whirlwind tour of three weeks. Horace's father, Frank Walker, was also present, still a strong climber at fifty-seven, and making up fourth man was George Mathews, of a well-known Birmingham climbing family. As guides they had two Oberlanders: Melchior Anderegg and his cousin, Jakob Anderegg.

The first problem was how to overcome the terrible lower icefall of the glacier where avalanches were crashing down almost constantly, as turrets and pinnacles of ice, some as high as a castle wall, collapsed under the relentless downward pressure. In this they were fortunate: two local men, Jean-Michel Lasnier and Julien Grange whom they engaged as porters, offered to guide them safely to the upper glacier by a path used by hunters and crystal seekers which avoided the icefall entirely. So the party were able to bivouac eventually on a small rock platform high up the glacier.

Ahead of them the glacier split into two branches, divided by a huge spur which appeared to lead up the face of the mountain to the ridge above, somewhere near the Mur de la Côte. This spur seemed their only chance of success, so appallingly steep was the rest of the face. But how to reach it? Whilst the others prepared the bivouac site, Melchior Anderegg went ahead to reconnoitre.

Despite the ease with which they had overcome the lower glacier, he had not changed the opinion he had formed in 1863. But, as Moore wrote later,

> seeing that upon this occasion he would stand alone, and that no remonstrance would make us abandon our purpose, he confined himself to indulging in observations of a Cassandra-like character, such as he thought calculated to check our premature exultation. His gloomy vaticinations had little effect upon us, and still less upon Jakob, who, notwithstanding his almost idolatrous respect and admiration for his cousin, ventured to deride his fears and chaff him generally in a free, not to say irreverent manner.

They knew their man. The big, bearded Melchior, built like an ox and with the heart of a lion, was renowned for his caution. One of the most famous remarks in mountaineering concerns the time an enthusiastic client pointed to the distant, unclimbed Zmutt Ridge of the Matterhorn.

'It goes, Melchior!' he cried.

'Yes, it goes,' replied the guide, 'but I'm not going!'

In this he was very different from his cousin, Jakob, a man in whom, according to Moore, 'prudence is conspicuous chiefly by its absence'. A handsome man, black bearded, Jakob was as strong as his cousin but he came to guiding fairly late in life: 1865 was only his second season and he was already thirty-eight years old. 'He had more dash and determination than any Swiss I ever knew,' wrote another climber of the time. On the Brenva climb, Jakob's character was to play a crucial role.

48

Top: The Mer de Glace winds its way from the very heart of the Mont Blanc massif. In mid-distance is the Géant Icefall with the Vallée Blanche beyond and the Col du Géant. Mont Blanc itself is on the skyline right, with the Aigs du Diable and below them in the foreground the Requin and the Chamonix Aiguilles.

Left: Edward Whymper, the young engraver who in 1865 with Adams Reilly surveyed the range and made several first ascents.

Above: The old inn at Montenvers built in 1840. The older shelter right was built by M. Desportes, the French Resident at Geneva in 1795 and dedicated 'à la Nature'. These served until 1870 when a much larger hotel was built nearby.

The Col du Géant and Peuterey Ridge. The Torino Hut lower left guards the col. Along the skyline *l to r*, the Aig. Noire, the Dames Anglaises and the Aig. Blanche. The Col de Peuterey is followed by the upper Peuterey Ridge to Mont Blanc de Courmayeur and Mont Blanc. Immediately left of the climber is the Brenva Face.

A climber plods up the Mur de la Côte to the summit of Mont Blanc. Behind him is the Col Brenva and Mont Maudit, with the Midi to the left and the Tacul to right, and the spiky crest of the Aigs du Diable, Miriam O'Brien's great climb with Charlet. In the distance is the bowl of the Talèfre Glacier with *l to r* the Verte, les Droites, les Courtes.

Melchior came back from his reconnaissance full of gloomy forebodings. He reported that between them and the Brenva buttress lay an icefall of unimaginable proportions. 'Such an icefall as I have never seen before!' he declared. He suggested that next day they should descend about a thousand feet and try to work a way round this obstacle, but the others didn't like this suggestion at all. For one thing it would bring them into the line of fire of ice falling from the séracs above, for another, I think they rather suspected Melchior's motives – any downwards move could easily be turned into a retreat.

At 2.45 am, after a comfortable night's bivouac, they said good-bye to the two porters, and set off to climb the Brenva Face, trudging across the glacier aided by the dim yellow circles of light cast by their candle lanterns. After two hours they came to Melchior's icefall. Huge pinnacles of ice, flushed by the dawn light, reared above their heads. Melchior had not exaggerated and yet, as is so often the case in the mountains, things were not as difficult as they seemed. A bold attack produced results and though, as Moore laconically remarked later, 'there was the usual up and down sort of work', there was only one tricky bit, which Melchior solved in his usual bold manner. By 5.30 am they were at the foot of the buttress they had set their hearts on; a distinctive feature now called the Brenva Spur.

The main difficulties – the icefalls of the Brenva Glacier – lay behind them. Now they would climb the spur to its crest and follow this until it merged into the easy upper slopes of Mont Blanc near the Mur de la Côte. Once there, they could follow the ordinary route to the summit and down to Chamonix. And this indeed is what they did, though not quite in the way they expected.

For two hours they climbed steep rocks towards the crest of the buttress, then paused for a brief breakfast, just below the ridge line. A fifty-degree ice slope took them to the crest and they were able to look down the other side to the glacier hundreds of metres below. They found themselves on a narrow but not difficult ridge of rock and ice which bore away left towards a pinnacle. They climbed to the pinnacle, only to discover that it wasn't a pinnacle at all, but the bottom end of the most fearsome ice ridge any of them had ever seen.

Fortunately, Jacob Anderegg, not Melchior, was in the lead

when they came to the ice arête: Jakob had neither his cousin's caution, nor his experience. 'He therefore went calmly on without so much as turning to see what we thought of it,' Moore wrote with evident relief.

The ridge was almost level and appallingly narrow: a horizontal blade of ice, where step cutting of the normal sort was not possible. Jakob, wielding his huge axe, simply chopped the top off the arête, and tip-toed along like a circus acrobat doing the high wire act. The others followed in similar fashion and soon the whole party was strung out along the perilous ridge. At one point it became so narrow that they were forced to sit astride it, *à cheval*. Moore, who was bringing up the rear, wondered what would happen if some of the party fell – would the others throw themselves over the opposite side to act as a counterbalance, and if so, what would happen then?

Happily, Moore's speculations were never put to the test. At 9.30 am they were all safely across the fearsome arête, recovering their nerves on the easy snow beyond. 'Do you think we'll get up, Melchior?' they demanded nervously. 'We must, for we cannot go back,' he replied gravely.

For the next two hours and a half they climbed up steep slopes of thin snow resting on ice which made the guides' work arduous since steps had to be cut most of the way. They had decided to make for the foot of the Mur de la Côte, at the depression in the watershed now known as the Col de la Brenva, and though they couldn't quite see it because of the intervening slopes they suspected it was somewhat over to the right. By taking a diagonal line they hoped to come upon their objective, but here again they were in for a shock. As they rounded a corner of rock they discovered themselves suspended above an icy cirque, 600 metres deep, which was the upper edge of the long Brenva Glacier. The direct way to the col was cut off by this chasm and their only hope of escape lay in climbing the slopes directly above where they were standing.

Unfortunately, however, their way was barred by an ice cliff of menacing proportions. The way ahead seemed impossible, the way back equally so. 'Our position was, in fact, rather critical,' wrote Moore.

It was at this point that Melchior's great skill and experience came to the fore. They were now truly committed to their climb and the time for doubts was past. The great séracs of the ice wall had to be overcome, dangerous though they were. He led the party up to the ice wall and then skilfully negotiated what was perhaps the only safe way through the barrier, turning this way and that in a masterly display of navigation and climbing skill. Today's climbers are agreed that it is this final barrier and not the ice arête lower down which is the crux of the Brenva Spur.

Eventually the difficulties were at an end. Moore's party emerged onto those gently sloping snow fields he had observed from the Mur de la Côte the year before. At 3.10 pm they stood on the summit of Mont Blanc and at 10.30 pm they were back in Chamonix, twenty hours after they had left their bivouac on the Brenva Glacier.

3 The end of the Golden Age

The years 1864 and 1865 were the climax of the Golden Age of alpinism. As far as Mont Blanc is concerned it was the time when the most important (or at least, the highest) of the subsidiary peaks were climbed. 1864 saw the conquest of Mont Dolent (3823m), Aiguille d'Argentière (3902m), Aiguille du Tour (3544m) and Aiguille de Trélatête (3930m), followed next season by Aiguille du Chardonnet (3824m), Aiguille de Bionnassay (4052m), Aiguille Verte (4122m) and Pointe Whymper (4184), the second highest summit of the Grandes Jorasses.

Five of these ascents were made by Edward Whymper, a young engraver whose ambition to be a Polar explorer had led him by chance to the Alps instead. He thought the snow and ice of the mountains might be good practice for the Pole, but after his first season in 1860 he caught the prevailing Alpine fever with a vengeance. To Whymper the difficulty or shape of a mountain meant nothing; he was a peak bagger whose only criterion was height. He would no more have wasted his time climbing inferior peaks like the Drus or the Chamonix Aiguilles, than Dr W. G. Grace would have captained a village cricket team.

When Whymper began his career the highest unclimbed mountain in the Alps was the Weisshorn in the Swiss Valais, but that was climbed in 1861 by Professor Tyndall. The Matterhorn became the new supreme challenge and so the ascent of the Matterhorn became Whymper's obsession; a struggle between man and mountain which in 1865 led to ultimate triumph and disaster.

Though the Matterhorn is the major theme in Whymper's career, his other ascents were notable achievements and none more so than in the range of Mont Blanc, though it was a region for which he had scant regard: 'It has neither the beauty of the Oberland nor the sublimity of Dauphiné. It attracts the vulgar by the possession of the highest summit in the Alps.'

The only reason he went to the Mont Blanc area in 1864 was

to help Anthony Adams-Reilly make a map. Until 1861 maps of Mont Blanc were wretched affairs which scarcely tallied with the features on the ground and even included a mythical peak, the Pointe des Plines. In that year, however, the great topographical survey of Switzerland being conducted by General Dufour published Sheet XXII which included the Swiss part of the Mont Blanc chain. Like all the Dufour maps this was brilliantly executed but, of course, it covered only about one-fifth of the whole Mont Blanc area. Adams-Reilly, a wealthy Irishman, set himself the task of mapping all the Mont Blanc mountains to the standards set by Dufour.

He began in 1863 and by the spring of the next year he had a map which tallied quite well with Dufour's. This he presented to the Alpine Club in manuscript form and so impressed were the Committee by it that they determined to publish it for the benefit of the mountaineering fraternity at large. Before this was done, however, Adams-Reilly undertook to cross-check it by making further observations from fresh vantage points. As his companion he enlisted Edward Whymper.

It was essential for Adams-Reilly's purpose that they should visit the furthermost corners of the Mont Blanc group and for the north-east corner they selected the Aiguille d'Argentière (3902m), which they first approached on July 6. Whymper had already been climbing in the Dauphiné Alps with Moore and so Moore, with his guide Christian Almer, joined them for the attempt. Whymper had Michel Croz as his guide and Adams-Reilly had François Couttet.

As they plodded across the glacier towards the Col du Chardonnet, from where they hoped to climb the North-West Ridge of the mountain, the day seemed perfect for their adventure. It was still and warm with not a single cloud in the sky. Yet the minute they breasted the final slopes of the col they were struck by a hurricane of wind, unbelievable in its ferocity. Against such a wind they could make no headway so the attempt was summarily abandoned. Moore and Almer descended the other side of the col into Switzerland to continue their journey to the Pennine Alps where they were due to meet the Walkers, whilst Whymper and the others retreated towards Chamonix.

Once off the crest again the wind dropped and the day was perfect. Whymper could not understand this but he came to the conclusion that if they could choose a line of attack which was in the lee of the mountain they might still succeed.

A couloir in the West Face seemed the very route they needed, so once again they turned to the attack. It was steep going but Croz was equal to the task, cutting no fewer than 700 steps in the ice. As they neared the top, the angle became even steeper, forcing the party to take to the rocks at the side of the couloir. Before long they came out onto the North-West Ridge about a hundred metres from the summit, where once again they met the ferocious wind. With the summit so near, however, they were in no mood to retreat. They started along the ridge, fighting to keep their footing as the wind tore at them; choking from the spindrift which it whipped into their faces. Their feet and hands became numb with cold and eventually, with the summit scarcely thirty metres away, they had to give up.

Having failed on the Argentière they set out from Chamonix next day to make an attempt on Mont Dolent (3823m), the south-east cornerstone of the range, where the frontiers of France, Italy and Switzerland meet. This peak is a long way from Chamonix, but distance was never a barrier to the pioneers of the Alps; the first night they spent bivouacked under a large jutting rock known as the Couvercle Stone (near the present Couvercle Hut), then next day walked up the Talèfre Glacier, past le Jardin, beneath the impressive rock and ice walls of les Courtes to a high, snowy pass, the Col de Triolet (3703m), which they crossed to the chalets of Pré de Bar in the Italian Val Ferret. It was the first time the Col de Triolet had been crossed.

Now at last they could see the mountain they had come to climb; a fine looking peak rising above the curious Pré de Bar Glacier. A long tongue of snow formed the South Face of the mountain and they climbed this without difficulty to the sharp summit. The views astonished them and Adams-Reilly was soon at work with his sketch book, noting the details required for his map.

It was, of course, a first ascent, and they were perhaps fortunate in hitting on immediately the only really easy way of climbing Mont Dolent. Nevertheless, the entire expedition – including time out for Adams-Reilly's sketches – took them only eleven hours. Whymper called it 'a miniature ascent'.

Nobody could accuse the pioneers of laziness. Having climbed

Mont Dolent and returned to Pré de Bar, they walked down the long Val Ferret to Courmayeur that same afternoon and next day set off up the Val Veni to attempt their next objective, the Aiguille de Trélatête (3930m). This was to be Adams-Reilly's observation post for the south-west corner of the range.

The peaks were shrouded in mist, so they spent the night in a shelter on the moraines of the Miage Glacier, 'a charming little hole which some solitary shepherd had excavated beneath a great slab of rock,' wrote Whymper. Here, too, they spent most of the next day as the mists continued to swirl round but towards evening the mists rose and allowed them to continue. Their route lay up a rocky gully of Mont Suc, which is the end of a long ridge stretching out from the Aiguille de Trélatête to the Val Veni. The climbing was not difficult but before long daylight faded and they were forced to bivouac for the night in a tent which they made out of their plaids. Today there is a small hut near this place for the convenience of those who follow in Whymper's footsteps.

They started out at 4.45 am next morning, following a snowy crest to a minor summit known as Petit Mont Blanc. From there they descended slightly onto a small branch glacier and then climbed the snow slopes directly in front of them to the summit ridge of the Trélatête. They passed over the East Summit (3895m) to the Central and highest summit, which they reached at 9.40 am.

Once again they were greeted with superb views which delighted Adams-Reilly. He was able for the first time to sketch the intricate detail of ridge and glacier on the south-west side of Mont Blanc. It was also, of course, another major first ascent.

When Adams-Reilly had finished his work, they descended to the Val Veni, crossed the Col de la Seigne and slept the night at the chalets of les Mottets in the Val des Glaciers. Next day, in a thunderstorm, they crossed the Col du Mont Tondu to Contamines and the Col de Voza to Chamonix.

Their tour of the Mont Blanc area was now almost at an end. They had more or less circumnavigated the whole range and had been entirely successful in their undertakings, with just one exception – when the strong winds of the Aiguille d'Argentière had forced them to retreat. It was typical of Whymper that he should spend the last few days putting the matter right.

This time they had no problems. Following the same route as

previously, they reached the summit of the Aiguille d'Argentière (3902m) on July 15. It was particularly gratifying to Adams-Reilly for it proved once and for all that the mythical Pointe des Plines, shown on earlier maps as being near the Aiguille d'Argentière, did not exist. He could now complete his map with confidence.

The ascent of the Aiguille d'Argentière was the third major first ascent of Whymper's tour. They had taken him exactly one week.

During this whirlwind tour of 1864, one peak in particular had caught Whymper's eye – the Aiguille Verte (4122m) which rises so magnificently above Montenvers and the Mer de Glace. He thought it would make a splendid viewpoint for Adams-Reilly, but the Irishman turned the suggestion down; he had, in fact, already tried to climb it the year before and found it too difficult for his liking. The mountain had a reputation of inaccessibility amongst the Chamonix guides, for what that was worth. Nothing was more calculated to make Whymper take note: he loved to succeed where others had failed.

And so the following year, Whymper returned to attempt the Verte. He had with him an outstanding trio of guides. First there was Michel Croz, Whymper's favourite guide, a pleasant looking man, sometimes impetuous, not known to suffer fools gladly and perhaps the best ice climber of his time; then there was Christian Almer, regarded by most of the early climbers as the finest guide of all and, finally, there was Franz Biener, who acted as interpreter between the other two since Almer knew little French and Croz little German.

They had already been climbing in the Pennine Alps before coming to Courmayeur via the Aosta Valley late in June, 1865. They were, of course, superbly fit and Whymper's plan demanded both fitness and expertise. His intention was not only to climb the 'inaccessible' Verte, but the Grandes Jorasses as well – the two highest mountains in the Mont Blanc range apart from the immediate satellites of the old monarch itself.

They began with the Grandes Jorasses, a formidably crinkled ridge which towers over the Italian Val Ferret. It was a day of boisterous wind with scudding storm clouds. Snow and mist combined to form a white-out, that ethereal state in which there seems to be no heaven or earth but just one all enveloping white plasma through which the climbers move like the ghosts of

Banquo. Underfoot the snow was powdery and treacherous, demanding great care, but at last they reached the summit ridge and at one pm gained the western summit, now called Pointe Whymper (4184m).

And here Whymper did what for him was a most unusual thing: he did not continue along the ridge to the highest summit at 4208 metres, but contented himself with the lesser top. For a man who was a confirmed peak bagger it was a most curious lapse and the highest point of the Grandes Jorasses had to wait for another three years for its first ascent when it was climbed by Horace Walker with the guides Melchior Anderegg, Johann Jaun and Julien Grange, and became Pointe Walker.

Two days later they set out from Bertolini's inn in Courmayeur to attempt a new pass over the mountains to Chamonix. The usual pass at that time was the Col du Géant, but this involved a very steep climb from Courmayeur (now done by cable car) and a long circuitous descent through the awkward Géant Icefall and down the Mer de Glace. The previous year, it will be remembered, Whymper had crossed the Col de Triolet on his way to climb Mont Dolent and it was probably during the ascent of the latter that he noticed another col between the Aiguille de Triolet and Mont Dolent which he called the Col Dolent. At 3490 metres it was over 200 metres lower than the Col de Triolet, and therefore seemed a reasonable bet for a quick passage.

But Whymper had a vague unease about the expedition even before they started. Because of this they left Courmayeur at the extraordinarily early hour of 12.40 am, reached Pré de Bar at 4.30 am and were on the crest of the col by 10.15 am. There were no problems on the ascent and it seemed that Whymper's premonitions were unfounded: at the rate they were going they would reach Chamonix by mid-afternoon.

It was when they came to tackle the descent, however, that Whymper's worst fears were realised. 'For the first time in my life,' he wrote later, 'I looked down a slope more than a thousand feet long, set at an angle of about 50°, which was a sheet of ice from top to bottom.' And he meant real ice, not the hard-packed snow which sometimes goes by the same name.

Croz, the supreme ice climber, came into his own. He it was who cut the steps for hour after hour down the precipitous slope, whilst Almer guarded the rear of the rope, prepared to try and hold any slip on the part of the others – though if a slip had occurred it is doubtful whether even the mighty Almer could have saved the party on such an ice slope. The descent took over seven hours.

It was ten pm before they arrived in Chamonix; a twenty-one-hour day which exhausted even Whymper who, upon reaching the hotel, fell asleep in an armchair. 'I slept soundly until daybreak, and then turned into bed and went to sleep again.' It was thirteen years before anyone else crossed the Col du Dolent, and that was in the opposite direction, which is easier. Even today, 120 years after Croz led his party to safety, the number of times the great ice slope has been descended could probably be counted on the fingers of one hand. The crossing of the Col du Dolent should have been the last time Croz and Whymper climbed together that season, for Croz had another engagement which he felt bound to honour. Neither man knew that scarcely two weeks hence they were to be reunited on the Matterhorn where like schoolchildren they playfully raced each other on the last few metres to the summit and where, on the descent, Croz and three companions fell to their deaths.

With Croz absent it fell to Almer to lead the attack on the Aiguille Verte. He had Biener with him and they employed a local porter to carry the camping gear as far as the Couvercle Stone, from where they intended to start the climb. Next day they were away at 3.15 am, climbing up the Talèfre Glacier towards their peak. Two hours later they came to the foot of a large couloir which soared up to the summit ridge and proved the key to the climb and is now called the Whymper Couloir. Almer was afraid of stonefall in the couloir, but there seemed no other way. At about half height, however, he managed to break out of the couloir, climbing ribs and gullies until at last a little ridge of snow led them to the summit. The time was 10.15 am. The summit, said Whymper, 'was a snowy dome, large enough for a quadrille'.

For a while they admired the view but soon the weather drew their attention. Large cumulus clouds were piling up, threatening a storm. As they hastened to descend, it began to snow, making the rocks slippery and the snow slushy. Their upward tracks were often obliterated and the swirling snow made navigation difficult. Great care was required if an accident was to be avoided, with the result that the descent was a slow, laborious business taking many hours.

They reached the safety of the Talèfre Glacier at 3.15 pm, cold and hungry. Eagerly they raced towards the Couvercle Stone where they had left the porter with their tent and provisions – and arrived just in time to see him about to make off. Whymper was furious; the porter observed that he thought they were dead or lost and was about to descend to Chamonix to inform the Chief Guide. As for the food, he had eaten it all, mutton, loaves, cheese, wine, eggs, sausages – enough for four people – with the exception of a morsel of bread, 'about as big as a halfpenny roll'.

It was not the sort of thing Whymper took lightly. Determined to make the porter suffer he set off for Chamonix at a cracking pace, his natural fitness fuelled by his anger. The two guides, equally fit, had no difficulty in keeping up but the poor porter, overblown with food and carrying the tent, was forced to shuffle and run alternately, chivvied by the others, all the way to Montenvers. 'He streamed with perspiration,' Whymper recorded with malicious delight, 'the mutton and cheese oozed out in big drops – he larded the glacier. We had our revenge.'

The climbing of the Aiguille Verte did not please the guides of Chamonix. Unwilling to give up their restrictive practices, they did not like the way in which foreign climbers, especially the English, had taken to importing Swiss guides for ascents which they regarded as rightfully theirs. They were particularly incensed that two Oberland guides, Almer and Biener, should climb one of the finest Chamonix peaks at a first attempt – a peak which many Chamonix guides had regarded as inaccessible. In the village that night there were some ugly scenes as the two Oberlanders were harassed by local men who accused them of lying. Next day the situation grew worse and there might have been a riot but for the intervention of the gendarmes, who threw the ringleader, a guide called Zacharie Cachat, into jail to cool off.

Within a week all criticism was at an end because the climb was repeated by Charles Hudson, T. S. Kennedy and G. C. Hodgkinson with the Oberlander Peter Perren and two Chamonix men, Croz and Ducroz. A few weeks later it was repeated yet again by Robert Fowler with Michel Balmat and Michel Ducroz (who thus became the first man to climb the mountain twice). Interestingly enough, all three parties used somewhat different routes to the summit – and this was a mountain which a few weeks before had been inaccessible.

Whymper's mission was almost at an end. There remained only one unfinished piece of work. He had still to find a satisfactory alternative to the Col du Géant as a way of crossing the mountains from Chamonix to Courmayeur. The Col de Triolet had proved too difficult and the Col du Dolent even more so. Now he determined to try the Col de Talèfre (3544m), which crossed the same ridge as the Col de Triolet but a little further south-west.

It was a case of third time lucky. Leaving Montenvers at four am, they arrived at Courmayeur ten hours later. The Col de Talèfre proved to be an easy and quick way across the mountains.

Whymper had finished with Mont Blanc. He turned his steps eastwards towards the Pennine Alps, where the Matterhorn and Fate awaited him.

The first ascent of the Matterhorn and the subsequent disaster is regarded as the end of the Golden Age of Alpine climbing. The details of the affair form what is probably the best-known story in mountaineering. It had no direct connections with Mont Blanc, of course, yet the shadow cast by the accident affected climbing everywhere for several years. The mountain was climbed on July 14, 1865 by Whymper, Charles Hudson, Lord Francis Douglas and Douglas Hadow, guided by Croz and two Zermatt men, the Taugwalders, father and son. On the way down Hadow, a complete novice, slipped and knocked Croz from his holds. Hudson and Lord Francis were plucked from their stances but Whymper and the Taugwalders might just have contained the situation had the rope not snapped under the strain. The four hapless victims plunged down the sheer North Face of the Matterhorn to their deaths.

To make matters worse, six other climbers died in the Alps that year – a total of ten in all – more than in the entire history of the sport up to that date. Suddenly what had seemed a healthy pursuit was seen by the public as lunatic folly; a foolish risking of life and limb. *The Times* thundered against it, the Queen was incensed. Partly, of course, it was the dramatic nature of the Matterhorn accident which aroused public opinion but what made it worse in the eyes of the Establishment was that the addicts of climbing were often leading figures in society, the Church, the professions or business. The Alpine Club sometimes seemed like Cambridge University on holiday.

Whymper was not the only climber active in the Mont Blanc range during the final two years of the Golden Age, though he was the most important. The easy Aiguille du Tour (3544m) was climbed in 1864 by C. G. Heathcote with M. Andermatten, and in the following year the neighbouring and rather more difficult Aiguille du Chardonnet (3824m) was climbed by Robert Fowler with the guides Balmat and Ducroz.

The last great peak to be climbed in that eventful summer of 1865 was the Aiguille de Bionnassay (4052m) at the extreme western end of the range, separated from the Aiguille du Goûter by the Bionnassay Glacier. Seen from the Tête Rousse it is a splendid mountain of towering ice and, since it is so visible from the Goûter route up Mont Blanc, one would have imagined it to be an irresistible challenge to the pioneers. But not so; the aim in those early days was to climb separate mountains, and they took a very conservative view as to what was and was not a separate mountain. Even leaving aside the many pinnacles which are today regarded as individual summits, some quite sizable peaks were dismissed as being mere buttresses to a grander mountain. For example, les Droites, les Drus and the Aiguille du Moine were at first thought of as simply part of the Verte. In the same way, the Aiguille de Bionnassay was regarded as an arm of Mont Blanc.

Such simplistic thinking was already leading some climbers to declare that the Alps were finished as a playground, for when all the peaks were climbed there would be no new challenges. Whymper, as one might expect, was of this persuasion and his later climbs were done in South America and the Canadian Rockies. Others, less blinkered in outlook, could see that if the rules were killing the game the proper thing to do was change the rules.

The other change which came about was more fundamental. Old peaks could be climbed by new routes. Some mountains like Mont Blanc already had two or three ways up, but generally speaking these arose out of a desire to find an easier way to the top. The new concept was to find a better challenge; the summit became less important than the way it was reached. This fundamental shift of emphasis was the foundation of climbing as a sport, for the challenge is open-ended and the climber, in the final analysis, can never win.

Over a century later it is fascinating to see the same metamorphosis happening in the Himalayas, now that all the great peaks have been climbed there.

The attempt on the Aiguille de Bionnassay was undertaken by three very strong climbers, with some notable ascents to their credit, E. N. Buxton, F. C. Grove and R. J. S. Macdonald, towards the end of July, 1865. Their guides were two Chamonix men, Jean-Pierre Cachat, a good ice climber, and Michel Payot, who kept an inn and was described by Grove as 'a publican, but not a sinner'. At first the guides strongly objected to the expedition because it was new and therefore not recognised by the infamous Bureau des Guides; there was no set tariff! But their objections were overcome and the party walked up to the inn at Bellevue, perched on the wooded ridge where the Mont Blanc Tramway now runs.

From Bellevue they had a splendid view of their mountain. Afternoon mists shredded against its icy flanks, emphasising the steepness and severity of the climb. They could see where falling ice and stones had fluted the peak with deep grooves: an ominous portent.

Leaving the inn at one am, guided by a bright moon and an incompetent porter who claimed to know the way, they eventually reached the edge of the glacier opposite the face of the Bionnassay. Close at hand it looked even more difficult and dangerous than they imagined: an enormous wall of ice, broken by crevasses and ice cliffs, scarred by avalanche debris and pitted by falling stones. Looking on the bright side, Buxton observed that there was nothing like a few showers of falling stones to enliven the monotony of a dull ice slope!

They chose a route somewhat to the right of centre on the face. There was no guiding ridge or buttress, just soaring ice through which they had to pick the easiest way. Cachat led splendidly, through avalanche debris and across blue ice. At one stage they climbed an ice rib so steep, Grove said, 'that I looked down between my heels on the head of the man beneath me, and wondered if he was standing on nothing, as he seemed to be'. Fortunately, the stonefall they expected did not materialise, nor did any ice break away from the upper part of the face, but it must have been a nervous time for them all. It took them five hours to reach the summit ridge.

Here they rested awhile, but threatening clouds soon made them start again. Snow began to fall and the wind rose to a fury as they battled along a difficult ridge towards the summit. The violent wind whipped the snow into their faces so that they were unable to see where they were going. Their clothes and hair became matted with snow; icicles hung from their eyebrows and beards.

It became obvious that they were moving into the heart of the storm. The roll of thunder grew ever nearer and presently their ice axes began to buzz with electric discharge, the familiar 'singing' noise which is the ominous warning of lightning danger. An ice wall suddenly loomed up out of the murk, which they climbed to a crest so narrow they were forced to straddle it, *à cheval*. (The summit was untrodden by human foot, remarked Buxton, laconically.) They had no idea where they were.

Then, for a few moments, the storm abated, the veils of cloud lifted, and revealed the dramatic nature of their situation. They were sitting astride a snow ridge either at, or just beyond, the summit of the Aiguille de Bionnassay. In front of them the ridge dropped in a sweeping curve like the blade of a scimitar, rising again to meet the Dôme du Goûter in the distance. It was sharp beyond belief and on either hand the sides of the ridge dropped in dizzying ice slopes. 'I thought it at the moment the most terrific thing I had ever seen in the Alps,' wrote Grove later.

It had been their intention to cross this ridge to the Dôme du Goûter and descend from there to Chamonix by the ordinary Mont Blanc route, but now they could see that the distance was too great and, in present conditions, the ridge too dangerous. As the storm clouds rolled in again, obliterating the view, the climbers considered their dilemma. They were trapped on an unknown mountain, in the midst of a storm and the afternoon already well advanced. The way ahead was impossible and, they all agreed, so was the way back. None of them thought they could safely descend the icy slopes leading to the Bionnassay Glacier.

Had the storm abated before darkness fell, they might have seen the ridge leading south to the Col de Miage, which is now the usual way up this difficult mountain. As it was, however, they decided that the only way open to them was to try and descend the South-West Face of the mountain which overlooks the French, or northern, Miage Glacier, though it too was completely unknown.

With the storm still beating round their ears they began an epic descent, starting with a huge couloir then, as that got too difficult, transferring to another, then another and so on for hour after hour. Stones began to whistle round their ears, though fortunately nobody was hit. At last, in the final remnants of daylight, they reached the Miage Glacier. The storm now blew itself out leaving a fine cold night with a canopy of stars but just as the weary party were about to bivouac a volley of stones from the cliffs above flew over their heads, causing them to flee to a more sheltered spot. Here they spent seven miserable hours, wet through and frozen to the marrow. They had been on the go for seventeen and a half hours.

The first ascent of the Aiguille de Bionnassay was an epic climb on a 'new' peak. It was not repeated for sixty years.

A few days later Buxton, Grove and Macdonald made one final expedition which drew together some of those who had taken part in the most memorable events of 1865. Young Peter Taugwalder, one of the three survivors of the Matterhorn disaster, turned up in Chamonix, where feeling was running high over the death of Michel Croz. In a tavern one day he was accused of cutting the rope (a rumour which persisted for many years) and when he walked out in silent indignation, this was taken as an admission of guilt. Buxton agreed to hire him as a porter but when they heard of this his two Chamonix guides, Cachat and Payot, went on strike. Cachat eventually returned to the fold but Payot steadfastly refused to rejoin the party. Instead, they were joined by Jakob Anderegg, the guide who had led Moore's party in the sensational climb of the Brenva Face of Mont Blanc.

The route, made long and arduous by much soft snow, was a crossing of the Dôme du Goûter from Chamonix, descending directly to the Italian, or southern, Miage Glacier and thence to Courmayeur. Some years later, done in reverse direction, it became the most popular way of climbing Mont Blanc from the Italian side.

4   The Young Turks

During the 1870s a new breed of climber was born in the Alps; one which had scant regard for the shibboleths of its elders (and therefore, in Victorian terms, its betters) and whose only use for sacred cows was to slaughter them.

Naturally enough, this did not go down well with the older climbers, including those who were old before their time. After all, the sport had only been going for some twenty years and the founding fathers were, for the most part, still active. But they had become set in their ways, and their ways were not the ways of youth.

It is true there were some very good climbers who followed more or less the traditional paths and did some very fine ascents – Freshfield, Coolidge and Kugy might be quoted as examples – but there were others who took a bolder approach: Middlemore, Oakley Maund, Lord Wentworth, Cordier, Duhamel, Boileau de Castelnau, the Zsigmondy brothers – a line which, by the end of the century, was to lead to the superb craftsmanship of Mummery and his contemporaries on the one hand, and the Nietzschean approach of Guido Lammer on the other.

And there were guides to catch the prevailing mood – Emile Rey and Alexander Burgener, for example, or even encourage it, as Johann Jaun and Ferdinand Imseng did. Ultimately, of course, many of the best amateurs climbed guideless, but, like winter climbing, solo climbing and women's ascents, this was nothing new. What was new was that more of them did it and at a higher standard.

The disquiet felt by the elders boiled over after a particularly hazardous climb by Birmingham leather merchant, Thomas Middlemore who, with Johann Jaun and a terrified porter (who spent much of the climb praying for deliverance) crossed the Col des Grandes Jorasses from Italy to Chamonix in 1874. Middlemore confessed to being black and blue from bruises made by falling stones and the traditionalists were horrified, not so much because he risked his life (that was his own affair) but that he risked the lives of those with him. In fact, it was Johann Jaun who had suggested the climb in the first place. A protégé of Melchior Anderegg, he did not share the latter's famous caution. Once when the great Melchior was shown a possible climb with an obvious stonefall hazard, he shook his head and remarked, 'I think we'll leave that one for Herr Middlemore.'

In his defence, Middlemore had this to say: 'Shall fools rush in where angels fear to tread? . . . The question is just this: nearly all the best things in the Alps have been done. What remains is stiff and possibly risky. How then shall we deal with this residuum? Some with, I am sorry to say, a certain flavour of official sanction, have counselled not simply caution, a thing which should always influence us, but have advised that the residual climbs, if involving possible danger, should be attempted by neither travellers nor guides. If this advice were followed, it would seem to me a cancelling of the indentures of the younger members who have apprenticed themselves to the noble pursuit.'

One of these tempting residual climbs was the first ascent of Mont Blanc by the Brouillard and Frêney Glaciers: the very heart of the complicated wilderness of rock and ice which guards the southern face of the mountain. It was an obvious but formidable challenge. As early as 1864 John Birkbeck Jnr had ascended the Brouillard Glacier and tried to climb the upper part of the Brouillard Ridge but had retreated, then nine years later the Rev. A. G. Girdlestone with W. E. Utterson-Kelso got no further than the head of the Brouillard Glacier after twelve hours of hard going from Courmayeur.

The following year, 1874, a very strong team took up the challenge: Thomas Middlemore was joined by T. S. Kennedy of Leeds with two guides, Johann Fischer – 'the strongest guide who ever lived' according to Kennedy – Johann Jaun and a couple of local porters. They made their way up the eastern side of the Brouillard Glacier, then, in bad weather, bivouacked for the night just below the crest of the Innominata Ridge which separates the Brouillard and Frêney Glaciers – and were somewhat chastened to see the route they had so recently been following raked by a sudden murderous stonefall. As next day the weather was still bad, they retreated, hastening nervously

66

through the stonefall zone to safety. Fischer swore that if ever he came again, another way would have to be found.

When Kennedy returned home Fischer joined other Leeds climbers: Garth Marshall, a young man in his third Alpine season, and his cousin Frank Marshall. In the previous two years Kennedy, Garth Marshall and Fischer had made the important first ascents of the Aiguille de Leschaux (3759m) and Aiguille de Blaitière (3522m) and had crossed a difficult col at the head of the Leschaux Glacier where Marshall had found some dead swallows which prompted him to invent the lovely name of Col des Hirondelles by which it was ever after known.

After a few climbs the Marshalls and Fischer were joined by Ulrich Almer, then only twenty-five years old but destined to become almost as great a guide as his father, Christian Almer. Almer knew them well, for not only had he climbed with them, he also had a special affinity with the Leeds group of alpinists. He had spent the winter of 1896–7 in Leeds, learning English at the home of J. H. Kitson, another Leeds man.

Together they traversed the Aletschhorn and the Zinal Rothorn before making their way to Val Ferret where Frank Marshall left them. From the chalets at Pré de Bar, Garth Marshall and the two guides proceeded to make the first ascent of the Aiguille de Triolet (3870m), then, after a few days rest at Bertolini's inn at Courmayeur, turned their attention to the Brouillard Glacier.

They followed Kennedy's route about half way up the glacier to a point where some grassy moraines gave a bivouac site for the night. This was really much too low for their purpose but no doubt Fischer wanted a full day in which to find a way past the stonefall danger he knew lay ahead. Exactly which way they went on the following day is not certain but they seem to have crossed the ridge onto the upper shelf of the Frêney Glacier and tried to climb the Frêney Face. Not surprisingly, they were unsuccessful in this bold venture. The savage face, dominated by its gaunt red pillars of granite, was not climbed until 1940! The hour was late and they were a long way from their lowly bivouac site, but they dragged themselves back over the ridge to the Brouillard Glacier and, aided by a bright moon, made a weary descent.

At about midnight when they were only five minutes from their bivouac site, disaster struck. The snow, which seemed so innocent in the moonlight, suddenly gave way beneath them and all three plunged nine metres into a crevasse. Almer was the lone survivor. Stunned by the fall, he regained his senses only to find himself lying in the bowels of the ice between his two dead companions.

At first light Almer managed to stagger down to Courmayeur to raise the alarm. Despite his bruises, shock and fatigue he insisted on accompanying the party which set out to recover the bodies; a long, sad business which involved Almer in another cold bivouac. Altogether he spent the greater part of seventy-two hours without sleep, in strenuous, traumatic activity.

One could be forgiven in assuming that the deaths of Marshall and Fischer would have had a sobering effect on any further attempts on the South Face of Mont Blanc, but nothing could be further from the truth. The route had defeated some hard men and had gained a reputation. It was the same motivation which many years later was to draw the best German and Austrian climbers to the North Face of the Eiger. The difficulties were a challenge; the danger they found acceptable.

The climber who took up the challenge next was James Eccles, a Liverpool man whose modesty was such that he left only the barest records of his climbs. He climbed extensively in the Mont Blanc area and always with Michel Payot, namesake of the guide who had climbed the Bionnassay with Buxton's party, but a far better guide, renowned for his ice climbing ability. Eccles and Payot became inseparable companions in the mountains for forty years, whether it was exploring the peaks of Colorado or shooting grouse on the Pennine moors. Both men were exceptionally strong but Eccles bowed to his guide's superiority in this respect: Payot had on one occasion carried an exhausted Eccles across the Col du Tour, together with their ropes, rucksacks and ice-axes. Eccles maintained he had only once known Payot display fear, and that was when he thought he was going to be scalped by Indians during their American tour.

Eccles and Payot were the first to climb the Aiguille du Plan (3673m), second highest of the splendid spires which dominate the village of Chamonix. They took what is now the usual route from the Géant Glacier – an elegant snow climb of no great difficulty – and thought so little about it that Eccles only gave a brief account of it many years later, by which time he had forgotten most of the details, except that it was early in July. It was the first ascent of any of the Chamonix Aiguilles since the Aiguille du Midi was climbed back in 1818. But the time for the Aiguilles was not yet come: the many rocky pinnacles which are such an attraction to today's climber were still largely disregarded. After the Midi and the Plan, the only sizable peak in the group is the Aiguille de Blaitière (3522m) which was climbed in 1874 and, with a couple of notable exceptions, the rest had to wait till the end of the century.

Meanwhile, Eccles continued to snap up unconsidered trifles left by the pioneers: the Aiguille de Rochefort (4001m), which he traversed in 1873, Aiguille du Tacul (3444m) in 1880, and Dôme du Rochefort (4015m) in 1881. He also tried, as did most of the young Turks, some of the 'last great problems' of the district such as the Grands Charmoz and the Charpoua Face of the Verte, but without success. These had to await the genius of Mummery – though Eccles might have succeeded on the Verte had it not been for a sudden storm.

In 1875 Eccles and Payot set out to reconnoitre the Brouillard Glacier. If the recce proved a success Middlemore intended to join them in a full-scale assault. They followed the route which Kennedy had taken but instead of crossing to the Frêney Glacier as Marshall had done, they turned west across the glacier towards a gap in the Brouillard Ridge now called the Col Emile Rey. The approach to the col was a steep couloir and though Eccles reckoned they could have climbed this, he saw no way of climbing the ridge beyond, over a buttress called the Pointe Louis Amédée, because the rocks looked too smooth, and the couloir was an obvious stonefall trap in the late afternoon, should they need to retreat down it. Eccles and Payot abandoned their attempt, which is a pity, because they missed climbing what is now regarded as one of the great ridge climbs of Mont Blanc, the Brouillard Ridge. It was left for a fine Italian climber, G. B. Gugliermina and the guide Joseph Brocherel, to complete Eccles' climb in 1901.

The two men now turned their attention to the ridge on the opposite bank of the Brouillard Glacier, the Innominata Ridge. They climbed up this easily to the ridge line, then to an adjacent small peak on the ridge, the Pic Eccles. From here they could observe both the Brouillard and Frêney Faces of the

mountain – and their hearts sank. There seemed no way up
either. Across the Frêney Glacier rose the superb triple-pointed
peak of the Aiguille Blanche de Peuterey from which a high ridge
continued to Mont Blanc, but this too seemed impossible. Somewhat disheartened, Eccles and Payot returned to Courmayeur.

In the autumn of that same year Eccles was walking down the
Strand one day when his eye was attracted by a photograph
in a shop window. The photograph was of the Peuterey Ridge
and though taken at a distance it showed Eccles that the upper
part of the ridge was not nearly as steep as he had imagined.
Standing there, in a busy London street, he let his mind's eye
trace a possible route to the summit of Mont Blanc.

Unfortunately for Eccles the weather during the following
season was so bad that there was no hope of attempting his new
route and the season after that, 1877, didn't start any better. He
crossed from Chamonix to Courmayeur by a new pass which he
called the Col de Rochefort (and as the canny Payot pointed out,
thereby saved themselves the two francs tax per guide that
Chamonix imposed on anyone using the normal route over the
Col du Géant), but the bad weather forced them to start back for
Chamonix next day. A week later another fine spell tempted
them to Courmayeur again, but the weather broke and it was
a further week before they could make an attempt. Even then
their luck was no better. They reached the Pic Eccles as they had
done two years before, then bad weather closed in and forced
them back to Courmayeur.

No sooner had they arrived back at the village than the fickle
weather changed yet again so after a night's rest Eccles once
more set off for the Brouillard Glacier. By now the party had
been joined by Michel Payot's younger brother, Alphonse, a
guide of little more than a year's standing, but one who seemed
to have inherited all his brother's fine qualities. Once again
they found themselves on the Innominata Ridge, where they
bivouacked. The night was fine and bitterly cold – they were at
some 3700 metres – and their sheepskin rugs, which was all they
had in way of sleeping bags, barely sufficed to keep them warm.
They were glad to make a start at 2.55 am.

Crossing the Pic Eccles they began a perilous descent to the
Frêney Glacier. A steep, narrow couloir swept down, flanked by
rocks which were, if anything, even steeper and coated with a

glaze of ice. Down these rocks they picked their way, then by the couloir itself, until at last they reached the Frêney Glacier.

It is perhaps worth pausing a moment at this point to explain why anyone should climb one glacier then cross a ridge to reach another glacier. Why not go straight up the Frêney Glacier in the first place? The answer lies in the nature of the Frêney Glacier, which is like a badly shaped hour-glass with one long bulb, the lower glacier, and one short one, the upper glacier. The neck between the two is occupied by a stupendous icefall which would be too dangerous to climb, and so to the pioneers there seemed no direct access from the lower glacier to the upper. In 1880, three years after the Eccles climb, a way past the icefall was discovered by the great guide Emile Rey, who led his client, Gruber, up a curious rock buttress now known as the Rochers Gruber. But even this isn't altogether straightforward – many years later, as we shall see, it became the scene of one of the greatest tragedies ever to take place on Mont Blanc.

Meanwhile, Michel Payot led his two companions across the bowl of the upper glacier, beneath the towering pink granite buttresses which form the Frêney Face, towards a steep ice couloir which sweeps down from the Peuterey Ridge. At the foot of the couloir they paused for breakfast, then began to climb, first by some rocks then by the couloir itself, towards the ridge. At five minutes past eight they stood on the Peuterey Ridge, having overcome what is now called the Couloir Eccles.

A narrow snow ridge, interrupted by two bosses of rock, swept up before them. Michel Payot, tired from step cutting all the way up the Eccles Couloir, now gave way to his brother, who led superbly to the first rock boss – two and a quarter hours of continuous step cutting up a steep ridge 'wide enough for one man, but not two' as Eccles later described it. At 11.40 am they had broken through the cornice which lapped like a frozen wave over the top of the ridge and stood by the shattered rocks which form the summit of Mont Blanc de Courmayeur (4748m). An hour later and they had crossed the easy slopes separating this peak from the summit of Mont Blanc itself, where Eccles was disgusted at the litter left by fellow climbers and their guides. They then descended the Bosses Ridge and reached Chamonix at 4.40 pm, some thirteen and a half hours after leaving their bivouac that morning.

This ascent by Eccles and the Payots was an outstanding feat on several counts. First, and rather surprisingly, it was the first ascent of Mont Blanc de Courmayeur, a summit which is quite easily reached by a stroll from Mont Blanc, but which, presumably, nobody had thought it worth while doing. Then too, it is notable for the times involved – six and a quarter hours of arduous step cutting were necessary, the route to the summit was over totally unknown country, yet they reached Mont Blanc de Courmayeur in less than nine hours. This is roughly the same time as that taken by George Finch's party when they made the second ascent of the route *forty-four years later* – and Finch started from a higher bivouac and wore crampons, which did away with most of the step cutting.

Most notable of all, however, was the fact that this was the first breach in the most formidable of all Mont Blanc's defences; the great southern ramparts which stretch from the Brenva Spur to the Brouillard Ridge. The more elegant variant which Rey and Gruber did three years later has perhaps more appeal and Eccles' route is seldom, if ever, followed nowadays because of its circuitous nature. But it was a major breakthrough for its day and it was a long time before anyone else was successful on this side of Mont Blanc.

A success of a rather different kind had been recorded a few years earlier, in 1871, when Miss E. L. Lloyd and Miss I. Stratton, guided by Jean Charlet and J. Simond made the first ascent of the Aiguille du Moine (3412m) – the first such premier ascent for women in the Mont Blanc area. Their route – a rock climb up the South Face of the peak – is not particularly difficult, but their ghosts must smile in satisfaction at the knowledge that it remains one of the most popular ascents in the region. Five years later Miss Stratton made a winter ascent of Mont Blanc with Jean Charlet, whom she later married, the family adopting the name Charlet-Stratton.

But it was climbers like Eccles and Middlemore who were setting the pace of Alpine adventure. I have called them the Young Turks because that invokes the spirit of their attack on the sport, though most of them were not particularly young – in their mid-thirties for the most part – and there is perhaps a mild sense of shock to realise that Eccles, for example, was two years older than Edward Whymper! Yet Whymper undeniably belonged to an earlier epoch and had little sympathy or understanding for the new breed. When the legendary Mummery died on Nanga Parbat, the *Alpine Journal* noted that his death was a great loss to the Alpine Club. In the margin of his own copy Whymper wrote, 'I do not agree'.

As far as our story is concerned the youngest of these hard men was Henri Cordier, a Parisian student of politics who numbered amongst his ancestors Ramond de Carbonnières, the first explorer of the Pyrenees. His career was short – four seasons all told – for he was killed in a glissading accident in 1877, perhaps brought about by his poor eyesight. He was twenty-one years old.

In 1876 Cordier joined Thomas Middlemore and J. Oakley Maund in a series of daring climbs based on the long ridge which joins the Aiguille Verte to the Aiguille de Triolet and forms the true left bank of the Argentière Glacier. Two principal peaks dominate this ridge: les Droites (4000m) and les Courtes (3856m), whose brooding buttresses frown down on the one hand to the broad Talèfre Glacier and le Jardin, from where they are usually climbed, whilst on the opposite side, the Argentière side, the whole ridge from the Verte to the Triolet forms a spectacular wall of rock and ice 1000 metres high and three and a half miles long.

When Middlemore and his companions came to this ridge there had been no ascents from the Argentière side. One or two climbers had reached the ridge from the Talèfre Glacier but neither les Droites nor les Courtes had been climbed. The highest, most impressive part of this long jagged barrier is the Argentière flank of the Aiguille Verte itself, where great couloirs sweep down between rock buttresses and the mountain's defences seem impregnable.

Johann Jaun, Middlemore and Lord Wentworth had tried the Argentière Face of the Verte in 1875, but it was a bad season which had left masses of soft snow everywhere and they soon gave up. Now, a year later, a very strong team indeed assembled for the attack. Besides Cordier and Middlemore there was John Oakley Maund, a rather quick tempered stockbroker who was making a name for himself as a hard man in the mountains, and to support Jaun there were his close friends, the indomitable Jakob Anderegg and Andreas Maurer, another Oberlander with a considerable reputation. Anderegg, Jaun and Maurer represented experience, intelligence and strength, said Oakley Maund.

They left Chamonix on July 30 during a spell of hot weather and bivouacked that night near the Chalets de Lognan, on the grassy alps bordering the lower Argentière Glacier. It was a beautiful moonlit night, described so memorably by Maund:

> The moon was rising behind the Dru and the rock face of the Chardonnet, where the bright light touched it, was silver-grey topped with the brilliant white of the snow. The glacier below us was swallowed in the deep shadow of the Dru itself. Opposite even the sterile, shadeless rocks of the Aiguilles Rouges looked beautiful tonight, and far away to the left the lights of Flégère and Brévent were intermittently twinkling out of the hazy gloom. There was that perfect quiet, that impressive stillness, which on nights like these adds so much to the grandeur of the scene, broken only by the soothing monotone of running water, or the noise of some falling stone, startlingly loud at first, but gradually dying off into hollow echoes, as it reaches its bed in the glacier beneath.

We tend to forget that an appreciation of mountain beauty often went hand in hand with the most daring adventures of the Victorian age, giving the lie to Ruskin's taunt that climbers looked upon the Alps merely as 'soaped poles in a bear garden'. (Ironically, Ruskin joined the Alpine Club four years later.)

They reached the glacier at dawn next day and were at the foot of the Verte by five. The huge face looked fearfully steep. On their left they could see a large pear-shaped rock buttress, flanked by a narrow couloir and more rock ribs, all of which seemed to lead to the top of the mountain, though they were later to discover that this was an optical illusion caused by foreshortening. The buttress was the safest way, beyond doubt, but an examination of the rocks showed them to be unclimbable, so Anderegg, who was in the lead, made for the couloir. Cordier was tied to Anderegg, whilst the others made a rope of four, led by Maurer. Jaun, freed from any actual climbing responsibility, directed the others as to which route they should take.

No sooner was Anderegg across the bergschrund than a stone came whistling down the couloir, narrowly missing Maurer's head, followed by another which skimmed past Middlemore. It was decided that the second rope would remain where they were until Anderegg had cut a line of steps across the couloir to the shelter of some rocks: to have all six men strung out across the couloir whilst the steps were cut, would be like setting themselves up as skittles in a bowling alley. Unfortunately, this left Maund in a precarious position, halfway across a fragile snow bridge over the bergschrund and he spent the next twenty minutes wondering for how much longer the softening snow would hold his thirteen and a half stone weight.

When at last they were all gathered together again, Anderegg led off towards the couloir, keeping clear of the stonefall channel. The angle was sixty degrees and the ice very hard, so it took them over two hours to climb ninety metres. Eventually they reached the rocks on the right-hand side of the couloir and, led now by Maurer, began to climb them until they were stopped by a smooth slab. There was nothing for it but to cross to the other side, risking the stones which they could occasionally hear humming down. They were successful, and in this way the climb continued, first on one bank, then the other, each time risking the stones which took the couloir bed as their natural fall-line.

After five hours of climbing they at last reached the top of the couloir and shortly found themselves at the end of a narrow snow arête, where they paused for lunch. At three o'clock they were on the summit, having accomplished a magnificent climb. But the mountain, as so often happens, had the last word. Their descent by the ordinary route towards le Jardin was done in a tremendous thunderstorm which brought rain and hail, making the rocks slippery and the descent miserable. They were barely off the mountain by dark and slept the night in a miserable hut near the foot of the Talèfre Glacier, after a strenuous twenty-two-hour day.

The route is now known as the Cordier Couloir and it was perhaps the most serious climb of its day. When Lord Wentworth's party tried to repeat it shortly after the first ascent they got into all sorts of trouble and only managed to retreat, frostbitten and weary, with the greatest difficulty.

A couple of days after their long day on the Verte, Middlemore's party set out again for the Argentière Glacier, this time climbing les Courtes by a very direct line to the summit and descending the other side to the Talèfre Glacier. They found it considerably easier than the Verte, but it was a first ascent, and another long day of twenty-one hours.

By now they had decided to complete the exploration of the ridge by climbing the remaining unclimbed peak, les Droites, no doubt spurred on by the thought that only three weeks previously the celebrated Anglo-American climber, W. A. B. Coolidge, led by the incomparable Christian Almer, had failed. In fact, les Droites has two summits, West and East, separated by a difficult ridge and though Coolidge had made it to the West Summit (3984m) he had not crossed to the East Summit, which is sixteen metres higher. Middlemore decided to rectify this.

Their previous explorations had told them that they were unlikely to succeed in climbing les Droites from the Argentière Glacier, since that was where the formidable rock and ice wall seemed at its most inaccessible. Their only hope lay on the Talèfre side. Consequently, on July 6, they set out to bivouac at the foot of the Talèfre Glacier, somewhat saddened by the absence of Jakob Anderegg, who was suffering from rheumatic pains brought on by the bitterly cold and wet descent they had made of the Verte.

Next morning they walked up to le Jardin and in the gathering dawn attacked the mountain by an obvious couloir. This they were forced to abandon as too dangerous when two big stones whistled past their heads. They chose instead a more complicated route over slabs which required some gymnastic rock climbing but which did eventually lead them to the summit of the East Peak, the highest point of les Droites. They built a cairn and left their names under it, as was usual for a first ascent, then after a while began their descent.

Because the ascent had been slow and rather difficult Jaun decided to save time by going straight down a snowy couloir which would take them back to the place where they had left some gear. At first this seemed a clever move – the snow was good and they made rapid progress – but as they reached a narrow part of the couloir they heard a sudden roar from above and, glancing up, saw to their horror two enormous blocks of rock bounding down the couloir, straight at them.

They made a rush across the snow for the shelter of the

crags bordering the couloir, but Cordier slipped and dragged Middlemore with him. Maund and Maurer jabbed their axes into the snow and fell flat on their faces, hoping for the best, whilst Jaun was knocked off his feet and fell over backwards. A second later there was a violent rush of air followed by a shower of snow particles as the two blocks came bounding over their heads, one of them missing Cordier by the merest fraction.

The only casualty was Jaun's hat, which went sailing down the couloir in the wake of the thundering rocks. It was a subdued party which scrambled out of the couloir as quickly as they could and descended the rest of the way by the slower but surer rock buttresses.

In the space of just one week, Middlemore and his companions had achieved three major new routes. A few days later Middlemore, Cordier, Jaun and Maurer travelled to the Bernina Alps where they put up two classic routes, the Middlemoregrat on Piz Roseg and the Biancograt on Piz Bernina. It was quite a season – and sadly, their last. Middlemore decided to give up serious climbing and young Cordier was killed on Le Plaret the following year. Jaun and Maurer, however, continued at the top of their profession for many years more.

Ralph Gordon Noel King Milbanke was a wealthy aristocrat and a grandson of Lord Byron. In 1862 he became Lord Wentworth and in 1893 succeeded to the title of Earl of Lovelace. He was one of the most dedicated climbers of the nineteenth century with a climbing career which stretched over thirty years – he made the difficult traverse of the Meije when he was fifty-six – and included practically every area of the Alps. He was known to all the guides as 'Herr Lord'. Though as a very young man he was active during the Golden Age, it was not until the 1870s that he came into his own: the ambitions and mores of the Young Turks were more to his taste and he climbed with many of them. He was particularly fond of rock-climbing, spending many summers in the Dolomites, and he once invited a couple of Dolomite guides to try their luck on the sea-cliffs near his Devon home, though nothing came of it.

Rock-climbing was becoming increasingly important in the Mont Blanc mountains, too, as climbers turned their attention to the spiky aiguilles. The rough scrambling ability which had sufficed for the pioneers was no longer enough; a degree of balance and technique was necessary for the newer routes. Some climbers, frustrated at their inability to scale difficult pitches, resorted to carrying ladders, a throwback to the early days when guides had carried ladders to bridge crevasses, but this was merely a temporary aberration which disappeared as skill increased. The guides too had to adapt to the new requirements: the tireless ability to cut hundreds of steps up an ice slope became less important than the ability to climb difficult rocks. All the famous guides of the second generation had reputations based on rock-climbing.

None more so than Emile Rey, a man who was a guide by choice, rather than necessity, for Rey owned a prosperous joinery business in Courmayeur and had been responsible for the construction of a number of Alpine huts. He was keen, intelligent, better educated than most guides, a first-rate climber, and Wentworth was unlikely to object to his fees, for Rey had a proper appreciation of his own worth and didn't come cheap. The story is told of how one day Rey was standing by the hotel at Montenvers when he was approached by a tourist who pointed to the Mer de Glace and enquired, 'How much?' Rey politely doffed his hat and indicated some guides from the Chamonix Bureau who were nearby. 'Those are the guides for the Mer de Glace,' he said. '*Me*, I am for big mountains.'

In his second season with Lord Wentworth, 1877, Rey made the first ascent of the Aiguille Noire de Peuterey (3772m), one of the most impressive peaks in the Mont Blanc range. It rises directly above the Val Veni as an almost perfect triangle of rock, whose arms are notched as if some giant had taken an axe to them. These ridges sweep down beyond the base of the peak to enclose a broad hollow known as the Fauteuil des Allemands – a possible comment on the width of German bottoms! The whole complex forms the end of the long Peuterey Ridge which stretches from Mont Blanc de Courmayeur to the Aiguille Blanche de Peuterey and finally the Aiguille Noire de Peuterey.

Wentworth and Rey were accompanied by J. B. Bich as second guide and Rey's brother as porter. They set out from Courmayeur just before midnight on August 4 and climbing by moonlight made the difficult scramble up into the Fauteuil by four next morning. The porter returned from here while the others tackled the rocks on their right, the East Ridge of the mountain. At first the going was easy, by means of a long rocky couloir now called the Couloir Rey, but this turned out to be something of a trap for they spent two hours trying to escape from the top of the couloir and eventually only managed it by some difficult chimney climbing. Once they reached the East Ridge proper they were impressed by the tremendous exposure, with steep drops down to the Brenva Glacier on the one hand and the Fauteuil on the other, but they met with no great climbing difficulties and reached the summit at two in the afternoon – to be greeted by a small rodent who slipped into a crevice as they approached.

They set about raising an Italian flag and Wentworth proposed calling the peak Aiguille de la Yola, 'after Madame Caccia Raynaud, an intrepid and accomplished Italian Alpinist then staying at Courmayeur'. Obviously Wentworth was very impressed by this *femme fatale*; let's hope he wasn't too disappointed when her name didn't stick.

They bivouacked low down on the East Ridge and returned to Courmayeur next morning without encountering any problems. It was altogether a very competently executed expedition, typical of Rey.

Rey's name is almost synonymous with the Peuterey Ridge, for though he never climbed the ridge in its entirety (that came much later) he was responsible for the Rochers Gruber route to the Col de Peuterey in 1880 and for the first ascent of the Aiguille Blanche de Peuterey in 1885. With Rey on this expedition were H. Seymour King and two Valaisan guides, Ambros Supersax and Aloys Anthamatten. Rey chose to ignore his Gruber route as an approach to the peak, since he thought it too dangerous, choosing instead the same route that James Eccles and the Payots had followed in 1877, except that where Eccles turned left to climb Mont Blanc de Courmayeur, Rey turned right to climb the Aiguille Blanche de Peuterey (4112m) – the last big virgin peak of the Mont Blanc range.

Meanwhile, on the northern edge of the range, attention was focusing on the Aiguille du Dru, a huge rock monolith which towers impressively over the Mer de Glace and is so eye-catching from Montenvers. It is actually a satellite of the Aiguille

Verte, to which it is connected by a high ridge which, with the Moine Ridge, encloses the small, steep, crevassed Charpoua Glacier. The mountain has two tops and that which the tourist sees from Montenvers is the Petit Dru (3733m), which stands in front of the Grand Dru (3754m), separated from it by a difficult gap.

Such a blatant challenge could hardly be ignored by the Young Turks. Most of them had a go at one time or another during the 'seventies, without success, but none more so than Thomas Clinton Dent, wealthy Old Etonian, playboy raconteur with the deeply affected drawl of an original Sloane Ranger.

Dent's climbing career began in 1868, when he was eighteen years old. In that year he made his way up the Saastal in the Swiss Valais to meet a chamois hunter whose elder brother was a guide, and who sometimes did a bit of guiding himself, usually with young people. His name was Alexander Burgener and he was twenty-two years of age; a huge bulk of a man, known locally as the Bear and reputed to be recklessly daring. The two young men hit it off immediately; both were ambitious, especially Burgener, and as Dent confessed many years later this led 'to certain performances on the mountains on which the writer does not desire to dilate at present . . . In those days we were not of an age very ready to take good advice.'

Before long the partnership began to bear more substantial fruit: first ascents in the Saas mountains and the first ascent from Zermatt of the impressive Zinal Rothorn. On his last climb they were accompanied by two like-minded companions, George Passingham, a gymnastics instructor and Ferdinand Imseng, a guide who was possibly even more daring than Burgener. Passingham, with whom Dent climbed frequently after the Rothorn, was incredibly fit and a very hard man to keep up with. For a while at least, Dent followed Passingham's practice of climbing everything direct from the valley, without the usual bivouac, starting early and walking through the night. Sometimes Passingham didn't even choose the nearest village as starting point. Whenever Dent had a long hard day he always said he'd been 'doing a Passingham'.

The long campaign against the Dru began in 1873 when a strong party consisting of Kennedy, Marshall, Taylor and the Pendlebury brothers, with five guides, made an attempt via the

Climbers traversing les Courtes, first climbed by Cordier, Middlemore and Maund in 1876. The traverse was done by Fontaine and Ravanel with L. Tournier in 1904. In the background are the striking Aigs Ravanel and Mummery, the latter so named after Fontaine declined the honour.

Above: Climbers descending from the Eccles Hut to the Brouillard Glacier. The Col Frêney is centre picture. James Eccles was one of the first to explore this difficult area on the Italian side of Mont Blanc.

Left: Victorian climbers below the Requin, first climbed by Mummery's party in 1893. The picture is by George Abraham, famous mountain photographer at the turn of the century.

Charpoua Glacier but failed even to reach the ridge which connects the Dru to the Verte. 'The monotony of the return and Mr Taylor's head were broken by the descent of a big stone,' wrote Dent later. 'This, Mr Pendlebury adds, with disinterested cheerfulness, was but a trifle. I have no information from Mr Taylor on the subject.' Shortly after this Dent and Burgener made their first attempt, accompanied by Passingham and the elderly guide Franz Andermatten, but they too failed. A second attempt three days later was no more successful. Both attempts, of course, were done straight from Chamonix.

In the following year Dent tried the mountain again, this time reaching the ridge which joins it to the Verte but getting no further. In 1875 he tried yet again without success, though he refused to be discouraged. 'The mountain is too prominent to be inaccessible,' he said.

About this time a metamorphosis came over Dent's life. He was twenty-five years old, idly rich, spending his time when he wasn't in the Alps playing sport of various kinds or cards. With his growing maturity he began to realise that he wanted to do something useful with his life. He entered medical school, qualified, and in the fullness of time became a distinguished surgeon.

He did not return to the Alps until 1878 when he once again set about the Dru. But the weather wasn't good, every attempt was frustrated and when September came round without any improvement in the prospects he decided to return home. However, a friend of his, J. W. Hartley, was remaining in Chamonix and Dent took the precaution of having Burgener remain there too – just in case the weather should improve. No sooner had Dent arrived home than a telegram came informing him that a miracle had happened – the barometer was rising and the weather looked promising. Dent hurried back to Chamonix.

With Hartley, Burgener and a nameless guide who proved useless, Dent attacked the Dru once more, but with the same success as previously. They had left a ladder on the peak with which to overcome 'impossible' pitches and much of their time seemed to be devoted to manoeuvring this into position. They retired to Chamonix but on September 11, 1878, Dent set out on his *nineteenth* attempt to climb the Dru. With him went Hartley and Burgener, with Kaspar Maurer, younger brother of Andreas, as second guide. The Passingham days, when he attempted the mountain straight from the village, were long gone and so they bivouacked for the night at the foot of the Charpoua Glacier.

They set off at four next morning, picking their way through the crevasses to the top left hand corner of the Charpoua Glacier which they knew from long experience was the way to the ridge they wanted. Soon they were tackling the intricate rocks. Their ladder, left from a previous occasion, was quickly passed and abandoned and they were on new ground. An awkward stomach traverse, where they wriggled like eels along a narrow ledge, took them to the foot of an ice-filled chimney at the top of which was 'a pendulous mass of great icicles, black and long like a bunch of elephants' trunks'. This was the way they had to go.

The use of the rope for rock-climbing in those days was not at all what it is today. Everyone climbed solo except in places thought to be specially dangerous, or if there was a weak member of the party. The guides went ahead, testing out the route for difficulty. When they came to a steep pitch they would climb it, uncoil the rope from their shoulders and drop the end down for the next man to tie on. At the ice chimney on the Dru this technique almost led to disaster.

The two guides started up the chimney, Maurer leading. It was delicate work bridging and backing up on thin water ice with hardly a positive hold anywhere. Suddenly, with a sharp crack, a great flake of ice peeled off beneath Maurer's feet. His fingers slipped and he began to slide helplessly down the chimney when Burgener, with one massive paw, pinned him to the rock. It was an incredible feat of strength on the part of the Saas guide – standing bridged across an ice-filled groove, over an immense abyss, holding Maurer single-handed.

There were no more problems, though the top seemed slow in coming. Dent could hardly contain his impatience. A strange rock arch appeared and through it they could see blue sky. There could be nothing above. 'Hartley courteously allowed me to unrope and pass him,' wrote Dent, 'and in a second I clutched at the last broken rocks, and hauled myself up onto the flat sloping summit. There for a moment I stood alone, gazing down on Chamonix. The dream of five years was accomplished. The Dru was climbed.'

The ascent did not go down well in Chamonix where, once again, some of the local guides refused to believe it had been climbed at all. They could not face the truth that because of their own restrictive practices, foreign guides were stealing all the best climbs. In the following year, however, honour was satisfied when three Chamonix guides, J. E. Charlet-Stratton, P. Payot and F. Folliguet made the first ascent of the Petit Dru entirely on their own initiative. As it turned out, it was a harder climb than its big brother.

After the Dru, Dent turned his attention more to the Caucasus than the Alps, but he continued to climb for twenty years more. As a medical man he had a natural interest in Alpine accidents and he it was who devised the mountain distress signal of six blasts on a whistle (or flashes on a lamp) in a minute, repeated at minute intervals, which has since been universally adopted and saved many lives.

Burgener went from strength to strength, his reputation matching that of earlier giants like Almer and Melchior. He was, everyone said, the best climber in the Alps and he would laughingly agree until one day near Zermatt, when he was with the great Austrian mountaineer, Julius Kugy, they spotted a tall, thin man riding on a donkey. The man's legs trailed the ground on either side of the beast. His back was hunched, his face pinched and he wore thick spectacles. He seemed so pitiable that Kugy was moved to compassion. 'Who is that poor fellow?' he demanded.

'That's Mummery,' replied Burgener. Then to Kugy's great astonishment added, 'He climbs even better than I do.'

5 Fred

Albert Frederick Mummery was born on September 10, 1855 in Dover, Kent, the son of a prosperous tannery owner. As a child he developed a weakness of the spine and he grew up into a somewhat ungainly youth, tall and gangly and increasingly myopic. Anyone less like a mountaineer would be hard to imagine – yet he was physically very strong, endowed with imagination, intelligence and courage. He had a lively sense of humour and was a born leader of men. He inspired people to rise above themselves so that no matter how desperate the undertaking, the issue never seemed in doubt. His strength of character seemed to vibrate through the very ether, provoking strong reaction; women adored him, some men hated him.

Yet the ungainliness of the child did leave some mark on the man. His weak back prevented him from carrying a rucksack and he hated to be photographed. When it came to climbing he was as hard as any man alive, yet he was by nature very sensitive, easily wounded by an unkind word or deed.

Mummery first visited the Alps in 1871 when he was sixteen, returning each year for the next five years. During this time he did some of the standard climbs – Mont Blanc, Matterhorn, Monte Rosa and so on but showed no exceptional talent. In fact, nobody had even heard of him until he suddenly reappeared in 1879, with Alexander Burgener as his guide.

Burgener's reputation was firmly established, for he had climbed the Dru with Dent the previous year, but he was temporarily without an engagement when this strange-looking Englishman, who was not even a member of the Alpine Club (a very desirable qualification in those days if you wanted a good guide) approached him with the startling proposition that they should climb the Matterhorn by the Zmutt Ridge. The route had never been climbed and would obviously be as hard or harder than anything so far done in the Alps. Burgener wisely suggested that perhaps they should try something a little easier first!

And so for a week they romped around the Saastal, doing climbs which were sometimes new, sometimes desperate, until eventually they returned to Zermatt, and made a dramatic ascent of the Zmutt Ridge – the first new route on the Matterhorn for fourteen years. It was obvious to everyone that a new star had arisen in the Alpine firmament.

Feeling that he had now proved his worth, Mummery applied for election to the Alpine Club in London. His record was better than that of many members; he was proposed by Clinton Dent, seconded by Douglas Freshfield, who was a Vice-President and enthusiastically supported. But he was blackballed in the ballot and so failed to gain membership. His supporters were stunned, Mummery himself was so deeply hurt that eight years were to pass before he applied again.

Popular legend had it that he was blackballed for being in 'trade'. His tannery in Dover was rumoured to be only a shoe shop, which was untrue. His rejection was attributed to the jealousy of W. E. Davidson, a very good climber but one not quite in the Mummery class, and certainly Davidson does seem to have been behind it all, but his motives are more likely to have been snobbishness. Davidson was an arch snob, a wealthy barrister who wanted the Alpine Club to be nothing more than a select coterie of upper-class friends.

In the background too, there was still a vague sense of disquiet felt by the older members towards the new climbs. Middlemore, Maund, Dent and others were members, it is true, but Passingham and Garth Marshall were rejected, T. S. Kennedy resigned over an election matter and Lord Wentworth, of whom even Davidson might have approved, withdrew his application at the last minute. It seems as though the Club, which had done so much to establish mountaineering, was beginning to atrophy.

But whatever the reason for his rejection, Mummery was undoubtedly hurt by it and there were times in the years ahead when he considered giving up climbing altogether.

In July 1880 Mummery and Burgener turned up in Chamonix after crossing the Col du Géant from Courmayeur where they had been prevented from climbing on the Italian side of Mont Blanc by bad weather. With them came little Benedict Venetz, a neighbour of Burgener's from the Saastal whom the guide employed around the farm and had started to take on climbs.

He was a happy soul, seemingly content to be the dogsbody of the party and the butt of jokes by his two companions, who regarded him as a mascot. Like Pickwick's Fat Boy, Joe, Venetz had the endearing quality of falling asleep anywhere at any time, given the slightest opportunity. Despite all this he was a very good rock climber and though Mummery and Burgener were no mean climbers themselves, when the problem seemed particularly difficult, Venetz was pushed into the lead and told to solve it. This he did without fuss, and climbing with Venetz must have been akin to chasing rabbits with a tame ferret.

Their objective in 1880 was to make the first ascent of the Aiguilles des Grands Charmoz, a savage stickleback of a ridge which forms the eastern end of the Chamonix aiguilles. The ridge runs north-south over a number of summits: Aiguille de l'M, Petit Charmoz, Grand Charmoz and Grépon, each higher than the last, until it drops to the Col des Nantillons, which separates it from the next mountain, the Aiguille de Blaitière. On the west it is flanked by the small but heavily crevassed Nantillons Glacier, whilst on the east it drops away to the Mer de Glace.

Even this description simplifies a complex spiky ridge where every pinnacle has its own name nowadays. In 1880 it was all called simply the Grands Charmoz and early attempts on the Charmoz were usually attempts on what we now call the Grépon.

Before Mummery came on the scene there had been a number of attempts, usually by the most obvious looking route from the Col des Nantillons, but these invariably came to a halt at a prominent ledge called the CP Platform, from the initials an early explorer had painted on the rocks there. Beyond it, the rocks were too difficult.

Naturally enough, Mummery's aim was to climb the highest summit, the Grépon, but before he tried that he thought he would try the slightly lower Charmoz because it had never been climbed and also it might give a fresh clue to tackling the elusive Grépon. A prominent rocky couloir separates the two summits and Mummery knew that this had been climbed two years earlier by Davidson in an attempt on the Grépon, so he decided to make it the basis for his attack too.

The Charmoz-Grépon Couloir is not at all difficult for experienced mountaineers and the surprising thing is that neither

Davidson nor Mummery used it to the full. Had they done so they could have climbed the Charmoz fairly easily, but Davidson was after the Grépon and Mummery was led astray by Burgener who followed a line he had once tried with Dent. This left the couloir midway and traversed left across slabs and ledges to a point below the ridge where the rocks steepened. Here they left every scrap of gear they didn't consider necessary, including their coats and boots, in order to be freer for the difficult climbing which they knew lay ahead. Where Mummery first learned this trick of climbing in stockinged feet (a method frequently used on British rock in later years) is not known: perhaps he invented it, or perhaps Venetz did. It certainly gave a much better grip on small holds than did the clumsy, badly nailed boots of those days.

Venetz now went into the lead. At first all went smoothly until they came to a twelve-metre chimney formed where a huge block had split away from the mountain. The rock was coated with ice and at four metres the ice bulged out ominously.

By patient wriggling on almost invisible corrugations in the ice Venetz managed to draw level with the bulge, supported in a most precarious manner by Burgener, who, straddling the chimney on tiny nicks cut in the ice, applied the head of his ice axe to his companion's trouser seat. Even so, little Venetz was not tall enough to reach over the bulge so he calmly requested Burgener to push the axe head under his feet instead, so that he might gain a few inches in height. This Burgener did, whilst Venetz somehow hung on to the ice with his finger tips!

This performance terrified Mummery, who was waiting below the chimney and he was truly thankful when the guides reached the top and dropped him the rope end. At the ice bulge he fell off, dangling like a parcel – probably the only time Mummery ever fell in his life. He felt mortified by the incident and referred to himself as 'the baggage' for the rest of the day.

But there were no further incidents and at 11.45 am, three hours after they had started on the couloir, they arrived at the summit of the Charmoz (3444m).

Or did they? Well, not quite. The various pinnacles which form the top of this mountain are much of a height but Mummery seems to have stopped at the wrong one. The true summit was reached by Captain Henri Dunod of the 12th

Chasseurs Alpins, six years later. Ironically, had Mummery gone straight up the Charmoz-Grépon Couloir he would certainly have reached the real summit, and with less difficulty.

The next few days were spent on a quick visit to Zermatt and another route up the Matterhorn, but on July 20 Mummery and his guides were back in Chamonix. They had put aside the idea of climbing the Grépon for the time being and turned instead to the problem of the Aiguille du Géant (4013m), which was the highest unclimbed mountain in the Mont Blanc range.

Even in an area which is noted for the striking appearance of many of its peaks, the Géant is something special; a huge finger of rock, drunkenly tilted, rising from a skirt of ice. It stands on the eastern rim of the broad Géant Glacier, which is the head of the Mer de Glace and since there is little to challenge it in the immediate vicinity, this isolated position emphasises its unique form. Freud would probably see it as the ultimate phallic symbol.

As early as 1872 the Young Turks were sniffing round it without success. T. S. Kennedy said in disgust, 'I think one might as well try to climb up the outside of a bottle.' Lord Wentworth, aided by the Italian climber de Filippi, got to a ledge within eighty metres of the top then tried the novel method of firing rockets with lines attached over the summit to a similar ledge on the other side. Unfortunately, only one rocket was on target and even then, the wind whipped the rope away. It is interesting to note that Wentworth was questioned as to whether using such extraneous aids was morally justified: an early example of mountaineering ethics, the subject which causes climbers more navel searching than any other.

But ethics were the crux of the matter so far as the Géant was concerned. Mummery and Burgener tried at least twice in that summer of 1880 to climb the peak, without success. At the foot of the climb Mummery left a visiting card in a safe place for anyone who might follow and on it he wrote, 'Absolutely inaccessible by fair means.' Two years later the card was retrieved by Alessandro Sella, who set about proving that Mummery was right.

The Sellas were a wealthy, politically powerful Italian family, responsible for the foundation of the Italian Alpine Club. In the 1860s Quintino Sella had seen in mountaineering a means of expressing Italy's newly found national identity and he it was who had precipitated the final tragic race for the first ascent of the Matterhorn. His nephew, Vittorio Sella, was destined to become one of the greatest mountain photographers the world has known but the rest of the family seemed imbued with a mountaineering fever in which conquest for the glory of Italy played a significant part. In such circumstances, ethics take a back seat.

In July 1882, four members of the Sella family, the brothers Alessandro, Corradino and Alphonso (aged seventeen), with their cousin Gaudenzio ascended the Géant, guided by three members of a famous guiding family from Valtournanche, the Maquignaz. Before the ascent proper began however, the Maquignaz spent four days preparing the route, chipping the rock to make holds (but only where the rock was brittle, Alessandro explained) and driving iron spikes into cracks in order to fix permanent ropes. Thus the mountain was climbed first by the guides, the day before the Sellas made their 'first ascent'.

Three days later the ascent was repeated by 'three Italian officials' and after that by a Signor Trombetta, all guided by the Maquignaz who fixed further ropes to the mountain. But, like Mummery on the Charmoz, none of them went to the highest point, for the Géant has two distinct pinnacles separated by a gap – the South-West Summit (4009m) and the North-East Summit (4013m). The Maquignaz climbed only the former; the higher summit was attained by W. W. Graham with Alphonse Payot and Auguste Cupelin about a fortnight later, using the ropes the others had left behind.

This is still the route by which the Géant is usually climbed, and it still has fixed ropes. Without them it would be much more difficult and, in fact, there is only one route on the mountain which does not use artificial aid of one sort or another, climbed in 1900 by a strong team from the Eastern Alps, where rock climbing had reached an advanced state by that date. Mummery was right though – in 1880 the mountain could not be climbed by fair means and as far as he was concerned, that meant not at all. He never went back to it.

Mummery and Burgener opened the following season by solving the problem of the Charpoua Face of the Aiguille Verte where Eccles had so nearly succeeded the previous year. It was a dangerous climb, made more difficult by ice on the rocks, but not one of special merit. He then turned his attention to the Grépon.

From what Mummery had observed during his ascent of the Charmoz the previous year, he had reached the conclusion that the Grépon might be more easily ascended from the opposite side of the ridge; that is, from the Mer de Glace side. Accordingly, with Burgener and Venetz he left the Montenvers Hotel at two am on August 1, 1881 and, picking his way by lantern up the Mer de Glace, turned the end of the Trélaporte Ridge until, working left over the little Trélaporte Glacier, he was directly beneath the Grépon.

Three large couloirs cut the face vertically and at first the guides tried the centre one but, finding it impracticable, turned instead to the one on their left. The bergschrund gave them some problems, but then easier climbing took them several hundred feet up the face. Gradually the climbing became more delicate, more time-consuming, so that after eight hours of progress they had got no further than the top of a prominent red tower. Above their heads the granite pillars of the Grépon soared up for hundreds of metres more; steeper, more difficult than they had bargained for. They could not possibly complete it and get down off the mountain that day and they had not come prepared for a bivouac. From the red tower, they retreated.

Mummery realised from this attempt that the Mer de Glace Face of the Grépon was much more difficult than he had imagined. It was not climbed for another thirty years.

So two days later it was back to the Nantillons Glacier and the Charmoz-Grépon Couloir. Burgener had never liked the Nantillons Glacier and on this occasion too he seemed to have difficulty choosing the correct line. Their progress was slow and soon they were overhauled by another party led by a famous Oberland guide. This in itself infuriated Burgener, who hated to be beaten even in so small a matter, but then the guide advised him not to try the Grépon. 'I've tried it myself,' the guide said, 'and where I've failed, no one else needs hope to succeed.' This was altogether too much for Burgener. He swore long and loud that he would climb the Grépon or die in the attempt!

They scrambled up the couloir until near the top, Venetz, who was scouting ahead of the other two, came across a huge slab of rock leaning against the side of the couloir and separated from it by a crack. Was this the way out of the couloir onto the Grépon itself? The crack looked like a severe test but Venetz put on the rope and began to climb. His companions watched, scarcely daring to breathe, as the little guide wriggled and squirmed his way upwards. Nowhere would the crack take more than an arm and a leg – his other limbs scratched for what purchase they could on the smooth slab. The first objective was a chockstone, jammed in the crack about halfway up, which he reached and grasped, gaining momentary relief. Above, the crack seemed even more difficult, but Venetz never wavered and finding some hidden holds, was soon at the top.

When Mummery's turn came he found the crack exceedingly difficult and wondered how Venetz, whose reach was at least a foot less than his own, had managed to lead it. In time it became known as the Mummery Crack, which is hard on little Venetz. It was to prove the key which unlocked the secrets of the Grépon.

The ridge on which they found themselves turned out to be extremely intriguing. First they passed through a hole which Burgener called the Kanones Loch, because it looked as though it had been shot through the ridge by a cannon. This took them to the Mer de Glace side of the mountain, but soon a stiff little chimney led them back to the Nantillons side where they came upon a sharp, slanting flake, which could only be climbed *à cheval*. This later became known as the Râteau de Chèvre – the Goat's Rake – though the only mountain goats to pass along it are human ones. Beyond the rake stood the pinnacle of the North Summit (3478m) which they soon reached.

They returned to Chamonix content that the Grépon had been conquered, but that night Mummery began to have doubts. The mountain has two summits, North and South, and though the northern one seemed the highest, it was by no means certain. He decided to go back and make sure.

Consequently, two days later, on August 5, they repeated their route to the North Summit, then passed beyond it until they came to a curious ledge on the Mer de Glace side which Mummery described as being 'suitable for carriages, bicycles, or other similar conveyances' and which has been known ever since as the Vire aux Bicyclettes. It took them to the pinnacle which formed the South Summit: a smooth granite spire, capped by a strange, flat stone.

There was only one obvious way up the pinnacle; a wide crack which looked less than reassuring. The crack was steep and virtually holdless, but Mummery saw that there was a ledge from which a rope might be cast over the top block to protect a leader as he tackled the pinnacle. He and Burgener set about this with a will, whilst Venetz dropped off to sleep.

But the target was small and the rope refused to land across it. In the end, utterly frustrated, the two men poked Venetz awake with their ice axes and told him that the crack would have to be climbed without the hoped-for protection. Venetz merely shrugged and set to work.

At first Mummery and Burgener were able to help the little guide by holding his feet in place and steadying him, but soon he was on his own, struggling up the smooth awkward crack whilst the others could only watch his extraordinary skill. Inch by inch he worked his way up until at last, with tired arms, he was able to reach for the capstone and pull himself onto the top. Burgener and Mummery gave yells of delight. Now the Grépon was truly conquered. It was Venetz's finest hour.

The South Summit (3482m) was indeed the highest point by a mere four metres, and the traverse, taking in all the famous landmarks, is now one of the great classical rock climbs of the Alps – though few modern climbers take the Venetz Crack on the final peak, because an easier alternative was later discovered round the back!

The ascent of the Grépon brings to a close the period of Mummery's first involvement with the peaks of the Mont Blanc region – and almost terminated his mountaineering entirely. In a private letter to Coolidge, then Editor of the *Alpine Journal*, he accused a member of the Club of trying to bribe Burgener and Venetz to fail on the Grépon. He meant his old enemy Davidson, who in 1880 had failed both on the Grépon and the Charpoua Face of the Verte, though of course Mummery didn't name him. Added to this he felt that the way Sella had described the ascent of the Géant in the *Alpine Journal* had belittled his own attempts. He felt once again that he had suffered injustice at the hands of the Club and since, in his heart of hearts, he desperately wanted to be accepted by his peers, there was an overwhelming sense of rejection. For four years, from 1882 to 1886, he did no climbing at all and when he did return, it was a very different Mummery.

In 1883 Mummery married Mary Petherick and through her, met three people who in their different ways influenced his life. First, there was his brother-in-law, W. J. Petherick, who was his first real climbing companion (apart from guides) once his wife had given up her own brief climbing career; then there was his wife's friend, Lily Bristow, who became a daring lady climber under Mummery's influence and perhaps something more; and finally J. A. Hobson, a schoolmaster with whom Mummery wrote a book on political economy.

When he did start climbing again it was with his wife and later Petherick, but they were easy seasons by his standards, though he did make two excursions to the Caucasus, a range of mountains then coming into vogue. But in truth from 1882 to 1890, Mummery was going through a period of change; it was as if he was searching for something within himself. Curiously enough, during this period, in 1888, he was at last elected to the Alpine Club.

Mummery returned to the Mont Blanc region in 1892. He now had something he had previously lacked, a close circle of climbing friends, of whom he was the undisputed leader. For Mummery it was like a rebirth; kindling again all the old enthusiasms, but in a new, more exciting way, for he had discovered the joys of guideless climbing. It was not that he denigrated good guides. He actually climbed with Rey and Pollinger during this period. But he simply recognised that no climber could be master of his craft unless he could plan and lead a climb without professional assistance. The responsibility was greater, but so too was the reward.

He was not the first climber to dispense with guides, of course: almost all the great climbers of the past had climbed guideless at one time or another but they had usually kept quiet about it, for it was thought of in much the same way as stealing jam tarts from the pantry. When a climber named Girdlestone blew the gaff in 1870 with a book called *The High Alps Without Guides*, in which he was honest enough to admit his mistakes, he was roundly condemned by the elders of the tribe, who conveniently forgot their own youthful peccadillos. In the twenty years since then, however, climbers such as the Pilkington brothers, Gardiner, Purtscheller and the Zsigmondy brothers had made guideless climbing almost respectable.

In the Eastern Alps university students were taking to rock-climbing amongst the limestone mountains of Bavaria and Austria, and since students have been hard up since the day the first university opened its doors, there was no money for guides. In England it was different: the toiling masses were still toiling, but the affluent middle classes – the same people who had discovered Alpine climbing a generation earlier – had discovered that there was sport to be had scaling the crags of the Lake District, Wales and Scotland. It was, they said, excellent training for the Alps and guides were unnecessary. It was this surge in rock-climbing away from the main Alpine centres which gave such an impetus to guideless climbing by developing both technical skill and self-reliance.

The group which now assembled round Mummery – Ellis Carr, Godfrey Solly, Cecil Slingsby, Norman Collie and Geoffrey Hastings – were all keen British rock climbers. The irony is that Mummery himself disliked British rock-climbing. After one visit to Cumbria he dismissed the climbing as being 'difficult and dangerous' and never went back, though paradoxically he sometimes climbed on the chalk cliffs near his home at Dover – perhaps the most dangerous rock in Britain. Even so, this powerful group – all chiefs and no Indians – accepted Mummery as their natural leader. As Ellis Carr once observed: 'Amongst Mummery's other mountaineering qualifications, not the least remarkable is his power of inspiring confidence in those who are climbing with him.' He also had an undoubted charm; in a rigid society where the use of surnames was almost mandatory, he was universally known simply as Fred.

In 1892 the first great climb of the season was not a rock climb, but an ice climb. The North Face of the Aiguille du Plan tumbles down towards Chamonix in cascades of steep ice, like a white ribbon carelessly tossed between the surrounding rock pinnacles. This long ice ribbon is the Glacier du Plan, which comes down the mountain to almost but not quite meet the Blaitière Glacier, which is a minor ice sheet at the foot of the rocks. When Mummery and Carr first planned this route they realised that the chief difficulty would be in getting over the steep barrier between the Blaitière Glacier and the Plan Glacier. They made their first reconnaissance on July 11; Mummery, Carr, Slingsby and Solly. As they climbed up the Blaitière Glacier the problem ahead of them resolved itself in brutal fashion into one of three choices. Over on the left, there was a dangerous climb which utilised a subsidiary glacier to overcome the rock barrier; but they knew that Emile Rey had tried this route twelve years before and had discovered it to be a blind alley. That left the choice between a long spur of rock which looked climbable but difficult, or a steep ice couloir on its immediate left which looked steep and dangerous. They chose the rock spur, and immediately found themselves with problems. Even to reach the spur was hard ice-climbing and the rock-climbing which followed was complicated and slow. Hours went by, the reconnaissance seemed to be getting nowhere and eventually time compelled them to retreat. And yet their mountaineering instincts had been right. Thirty-two years later this was the route by which a brilliant French party made the first ascent.

Solly's holiday was now at an end, but on the following afternoon the remaining three, Mummery, Slingsby and Carr, climbed up the steep slopes through the woods above Chamonix towards the foot of the mountain they had set their hearts on. Their intention was to camp as near the peak as possible and thereby get a good start the following morning, but in this they were frustrated by an incompetent porter who was carrying the camping gear and making heavy weather of the toilsome slopes. In the end they camped near the Nantillons Glacier, well short of their objective.

They were away by three next morning, soon crunching steadily up the now familiar Blaitière Glacier, under a fine night sky full of stars. A bright moon lighted their way. Ahead of them, like a silver streak, they could see the couloir which they had decided was the only way past the dark rock barrier. It was, they estimated, about a thousand feet high, inclined at an angle of something between thirty and fifty degrees. They reached its foot at dawn.

A closer inspection now showed that the couloir was divided for about half its height by a rib of rock down the middle above which it seemed to steepen considerably. At the top they could see menacing séracs, poised to crash down the couloir like waste down a rubbish chute. If the séracs fell whilst the climbers were in the couloir there would be no escape, but sometimes séracs can remain poised for years, and in any case there was no other way.

They crossed the bergschrund hard by the left-hand wall of the couloir, then traversed delicately across the ice to the central rock rib. This turned out to be both steep and loose, but it was quicker than climbing the ice and relatively safe from any falling missiles, so they kept with it until it petered out, pausing only to snatch a light breakfast at a convenient resting place. When the rib ended they found they had a choice of following either a right- or left-hand branch of the couloir and they unhesitatingly chose the latter as the safer of the two. For hour after hour, with occasional changes in leadership to share the burden of step cutting, they climbed the couloir's icy bed.

The angle of ascent was a fairly uniform fifty degrees but about thirty metres from the top, it suddenly steepened in a dramatic fashion to sixty or seventy degrees. They paused to consider their position. On their left the rock wall of the couloir bulged with wet overhangs, on their right lay the other branch of the couloir which they had agreed was suicidal. Either they must tackle the steeper ice or retreat. Mummery announced that he was prepared to lead it. They arranged the ropes to allow him a long run-out and he set off.

He was soon reduced to cutting steps single-handed, hanging on to the ice with his left hand in holds he cut specially for that purpose. He was directing his efforts towards a single projecting rock at the head of the couloir and as he approached it the ice steepened still further until for the last twelve or fourteen feet it was virtually perpendicular. The strain on Mummery's arms was enormous, yet never once did he falter: it was, said Carr, 'the most extraordinary feat of mountaineering skill and nerve it has ever been my privilege to witness'.

Mummery reached the rock knob, only to find it was a false friend. There was no rest there. So he was forced to continue, more easily now, until at last he had run out all 120 feet of the rope and was forced to halt. He cut a stance in the ice and brought up the other two. The pitch had taken him two hours and was probably the most difficult single ice pitch ever attempted in the Alps at that time.

A little further on they found a rock platform which gave them

e great ridges on the south side of Mont Blanc often terminate in superb rock peaks. Here bad weather puts powder snow on
Aig. Noire. In the foreground is the East Face of the Aig. de la Brenva where Mlle N. Pietrasanta and G. Boccalatte put up a
ous route in 1935. The sharp needle right is the Père Eternel, 60 m high.

Above: The Chamonix Aiguilles rise over the Mer de Glace. Extreme right the arrow-point Aig. de la République is follow by the more level seeming crest of the Charmoz and the dark curve of the Grépon. Young's East Face route follows almost exactly the line between light and shade. The main peaks left the Grépon are Blaitière, Fou, Caiman, Crocodile and Plan.

Left: Fred Mummery climbing the Mummery Crack on the Grépon, a picture taken by Lily Bristow during 'an easy day f lady'.

some rest and enabled them to snatch another morsel of food, then it was on again, up the unremitting ice, with Mummery still in the lead. Another rib of rock helped them on their way for about twenty-four metres, but then it was back onto the ice again, chopping step after remorseless step. Above them the Glacier du Plan continued in crest upon crest, shattered séracs poised like dragon's teeth.

To avoid the worst of the séracs they tried to veer away to the left towards a subsidiary summit of the Plan which is nowadays called the Dent du Crocodile, but they found the rocks extremely difficult and there were still ice patches, so that the arm-aching step cutting still had to be endured. Daylight faded into dusk.

When darkness eventually brought them to a halt the three men gathered on a tiny ledge, knowing they had to face an uncomfortable bivouac. They had not come prepared for such an eventuality; so confident had they been that they would climb the Plan in a day that they had left their extra clothing in their tent, far below. They wore only the sort of jackets a man might wear for a day on the grouse moors of Yorkshire. 'The coat I was wearing was not lined,' Carr observed later. Had the weather turned bad they would almost certainly have died from exposure. As it was they suffered acutely as the temperature plummeted, the kindly Slingsby hugging the frail form of Mummery to protect it from the shuddering cold. In the valley below they could see the lights of Chamonix, only two or three hours from the mountain but as good as a million miles away.

It was three weary men who turned to face the Plan again next day. They had nothing to drink, little to eat and the cold had gnawed into their bones. The very rope itself was frozen into intractable kinks. For a little while they continued their climb, which got no easier, but then Carr, all in, cried halt. Perched on the steep ice, they held a council of war.

To go on or to retreat? Could they retreat? Mummery was for pressing on. He took off the rope and began a daring solo reconnaissance, only to return shortly with the news that the mountain seemed unrelenting. At five am they turned and started their perilous descent.

Slingsby went down first, then the weary Carr, and finally Mummery, who acted as anchor. They had hoped to use the steps won with such difficulty on the ascent, but wind-blown snow and melt water had ruined most of them and they had to be carefully refashioned with blows from Slingsby's ice axe. For hour after hour this indomitable Yorkshireman bent to his task, pausing only to murmur, 'It certainly is a glorious climb.'

They realised, of course, that the crux of their entire descent would come at the top of the introductory couloir; that vertical ice wall which Mummery had climbed so brilliantly only the day before. The thought of descending it filled them with apprehension and for a moment they considered trying to escape down the rock rib they had reconnoitred with Solly, but in the end decided it was better to court the Devil they knew rather than one they didn't.

At the head of the couloir they tied off the rope on a rock spike as a sort of anchor whilst Carr and Slingsby lowered Mummery over the lip of the ice. He went down slowly, refashioning the hand and footholds of yesterday. It took him an hour before he was able to rejoin the others. Then Carr was lowered down to a safe place, followed by Slingsby. When Mummery's turn came, they expected him simply to swarm down the tied-off rope, which could then be abandoned as surplus to requirements, for rope they had in plenty. But Mummery would have none of this. Instead he descended the ice wall as calmly as a housepainter descends a ladder: the privations of the last two days seem not to have affected him at all.

The rest of the descent went easily enough, though Carr was cut by a falling stone. They reached the Blaitière Glacier at 5.55 pm and rejoined their anxiously waiting friends at Montenvers at 10.30 pm, just fifty-four hours after they had set out.

This attempt on the North Face of the Plan by Mummery and his companions ranks with the Cordier Couloir of the Verte as being one of the earliest climbs in the modern idiom. The face was eventually climbed by Jacques Lagarde, J. de Lepiney and H. de Ségogne in 1924. As far as the Plan was concerned, Mummery was thirty years ahead of his time. Later that same year he joined the great Emile Rey on an attempt to climb the Hirondelles Ridge of the Grandes Jorasses, and failed on that too – it was climbed thirty-five years later.

These failures of Mummery demonstrate how far ahead he could see the development of climbing and his eagerness to push it on. Even those routes on which he was successful were ahead of anything else at the time – take the history of the Grépon, for example; since Mummery's ascent with Burgener in 1881, nobody had repeated his route. What had happened instead was that the French climber Henri Dunod had succeeded in climbing it by the old CP route in 1885, and since his guides were Chamonix men this became the accepted way, though in fact there were only three other ascents up to 1892, including the first guideless ascent by Gibson, Wicks, Morse and Pasteur in that year. Scarcely three weeks later Mummery decided to put the matter right: with Hastings, Collie and Pasteur he repeated his climb by the Mummery Crack, traversed the mountain and descended the CP route, so making the first complete traverse of the peak and the climb by which it is usually done these days.

He showed too a modern outlook towards women climbers. Lady alpinists, as they were then called, were by no means uncommon but with a few notable exceptions most of them tended to confine their activities to the easier routes. Mummery showed that they were quite capable of climbing the hardest rock climbs of the day, given the opportunity. He led a large happy party which included Lily Bristow and Miss Pasteur in a traverse of the Charmoz in 1892 and in the following year repeated his traverse of the Grépon with Miss Bristow and Slingsby.

Indeed, Lily Bristow regarded Mummery as standing next to God in her pantheon. She was a tom-boy who bivouacked unchaperoned with 'the boys' and was with Mummery on some of the hardest climbs of the day, although, much to her chagrin, he would never take her on a difficult first ascent attempt. She climbed with Mummery in 1892 and 1893 and she it was who provoked him into quoting Leslie Stephen's dictum that even the hardest climbs eventually became 'an easy day for a lady'. But at the end of the 1893 season it seems that Mrs Mummery put her foot down, and Lily never climbed with Fred again.

In between the climbs with Lily in 1893 Mummery had climbed the West Face of the Plan, with Slingsby, Hastings and Collie, when they were able to see just how near they had been to success in their attempt on the North Face the previous year. Another three hours would have seen them to the top. With the same three companions, too, he made the first ascent of a sharp little peak overlooking the Géant Icefall, which had no name but which Collie christened Dent du Requin (Shark's Tooth), now one of the most popular climbs in the area.

All of these climbs, with the exception of the North Face of the Plan, were rock climbs and most of them were easily accessible. Mummery hated walking because without his thick spectacles he was as blind as a bat, yet vanity caused him to hate the spectacles too. So he stumbled his way up the rocky mountain paths, looking anything but the great mountaineer he was. Nevertheless, he had done some expeditionary climbs in the Caucasus, which involved long walks, and he had his heart set on the Himalaya for 1895. Perhaps this is why, in 1894, he changed tactics and instead of rock climbs, concentrated on big mountain ascents in the grand manner. With Collie and Hastings he made the first guideless ascent of the Brenva Spur; a climb which, perhaps more than any other, signalled that guideless climbing was indeed come of age. The same party then went on to climb the Verte by the Moine Ridge, which they thought was new, but was in fact Hudson and Kennedy's route of 1865.

A few days later Mummery returned to the Matterhorn to repeat the Zmutt Ridge, the climb which had first made him famous fifteen years earlier. Ironically, it also proved to be his last Alpine climb. In the following year, 1895, Fred Mummery was killed attempting the Himalayan giant, Nanga Parbat. Sadly, he led the way in this too: many more climbers would die on Nanga Parbat before it was finally climbed in 1953.

6   Twilight of the gods

As the nineteenth century drew to a close Chamonix was little changed from what it had been forty or fifty years earlier. There were more hotels – fifteen by 1896 – some tourist shops selling rock crystals and the Tairraz family had opened their famous photographic studio. But it was still essentially a remote Alpine village, reached only after considerable effort. For a long time the railway went no further than Geneva, where, after the overnight train from Paris, passengers would embark on the seven o'clock diligence for Chamonix. This cumbersome carriage, pulled by six strong horses, took ten or eleven hours to reach its destination, where its arrival at the Post Office was the highlight of the day, greeted by such guides and visitors who were not on excursions. Passengers going on to Montenvers hurriedly transferred their baggage to waiting mules and set off at once up the steep path so that they would reach the hotel before dark, and in time for dinner.

The mountains too had not changed much. The popular paths were a little more worn, perhaps, and there was a decent hotel at Montenvers, overlooking the Mer de Glace, but there were very few huts for climbers. The best was that on the Grands Mulets which had been rebuilt in 1853 to 'provide all the ordinary necessities of life', and there was the one Rey had built on the Col du Géant. Less comfortable habitations existed on the Aiguille du Goûter, Col du Midi and Pierre à Béranger. The glaciers, which had given the district its name in the previous century, were still in their full glory. Charles Pasteur, who traversed the Grépon with Mummery, described them as they then were:

I remember coming to Chamonix by diligence in my school days when the Glacier des Bossons was less than 100 yards from the high road from les Houches to Chamonix. The Mer de Glace then came right down below the Chapeau over the

101

Rochers Rouges. There is no doubt that these advancing glaciers added greatly to the beauty of the valley, with blue ice showing up against the fields and woods instead of grey moraine.

All this was coming to an end, as the glaciers retreated and the railways advanced. During the 1890s the railway reached Cluses, then Le Fayet, avoiding Geneva entirely, where the Swiss had the annoying habit of levying import duty on things like ropes and ice axes. In 1901 the railway line, electrified, was pushed on to Chamonix where a station was built in the fields just beyond the English church, on the east bank of the river. As most of the village lay on the west bank, there was a steady infilling between the old village and the station over the coming years. In 1908 the cog railway was built up to Montenvers; sturdy little steam engines pushing single carriages up the steep incline in what was rightly seen at the time as a marvellous feat of engineering.

Thirty years earlier Sir Leslie Stephen had called the Alps the playground of Europe, but in those still innocent days he didn't realise just what a playground it would become. He thought only in terms of mountaineering and at the turn of the century mountaineering was still the principal activity associated with Chamonix and similar Alpine centres. Winter sports such as tobogganing and skating were much less important, if only because there was no money in it. Then, in 1896, a wealthy Chamoniard named Dr Michel Payot introduced skis to the valley.

By 1901 Payot was organising instructional courses in skiing at the Col du Balme and Col de Voza. Others soon joined in his enthusiasm for this novel mode of travel, including the two guides Joseph Simond and Joseph Ravanel and with these companions Payot made the first ski crossing of the Col du Géant in 1902, descended the Vallée Blanche from the Col du Midi in 1903 and in that same year traversed the Haute Route from Chamonix to Zermatt. In 1908 Chamonix held the first international skiing championships, though sadly Dr Payot, who was the organiser of the event, had caught a chill and died from pneumonia just as the championships were about to start. He was thirty-eight years old. Sixteen years later, in 1924, the first ever Winter Olympic Games were held at Chamonix.

Skiing has long since replaced climbing as the principal sport in these mountains. Today's guides are also ski instructors and usually earn more in winter than in summer and if skiing plays little part in our story of Mont Blanc, it must never be forgotten that its effects on the environment have been profound.

In the last decade of the nineteenth century, however, mountaineering was still the king of sports. There were 303 registered guides in the valley, twenty-one more at Courmayeur and sundry others in the Val Montjoie, Swiss Val Ferret and Champex. From Chamonix the most expensive climb was the Aiguille du Dru which cost 130 francs per guide, whilst the Géant, Verte and Mont Blanc itself cost 100 francs. Courmayeur prices tended to be cheaper – the Géant, for example, costing seventy francs – although some of the more serious routes, such as the Brenva Spur and Aiguille Blanche de Peuterey were 'subject to special arrangement'. Charges like these seldom applied to the best guides, however, because they tended to have long engagements on a regular seasonal basis with the same 'monsieur'. A guide who for some reason lost his regular 'monsieur' was the subject of sideways glances and clacking tongues.

Although climbers had long since given up pretending that their chief interest was the pursuit of natural science, the ghost of de Saussure was not entirely forgotten. In 1887 Joseph Vallot of Paris spent three days and nights camped on the summit of Mont Blanc making meteorological and other scientific observations. He was accompanied by a M. Richard and two guides and it was the first time anyone had camped on the summit since Professor Tyndall, who spent a night there in 1859. Rather curiously, both parties seemed to suffer from severe mountain sickness during the ascent, yet during the hundreds of ascents made since Paccard and Balmat climbed the mountain, little mention had been made of mountain sickness. Perhaps it was not recognised – it is still not fully understood – but any doubts about the serious effects high altitude can have on the human body were shortly to disappear in dramatic fashion.

Vallot was so encouraged by his three days on Mont Blanc that he began to think in terms of a permanent observatory high on the mountain. This would allow for the continuity of observation which is so often essential for valid scientific results. At first he considered a cave, excavated in the highest rocks, but he soon abandoned this idea for that of a strong wooden hut built on a conspicuous rock outcrop at the foot of the Bosses Ridge. In order to do this he first of all had to obtain permission from the Commune of Chamonix, who actually owned all this side of Mont Blanc – and the Commune were not at all keen. They viewed Vallot's motives with suspicion. Suppose he opened his hut to tourists who wished to stay overnight? Would that not be detrimental to the hut at Grands Mulets, the lease of which was in the hands of the Commune? In the end, Vallot was allowed his observatory on condition that he also built a refuge at his own expense which would become the property of the Commune. Anyone using it would pay a tax of ten francs; one half of which would go to the maintenance of the hut and the rest as compensation to the guardian of the Grands Mulets hut. And so there came into being the Refuge Vallot, an emergency shelter which has played a crucial role in saving lives ever since. The original structure has been replaced since Vallot's day, but, now as then, the authorities have considerable difficulty collecting any tax!

Meanwhile, Vallot got on with building his observatory. He had some difficulty obtaining sufficient guides and porters because construction could only take place in high summer, when, of course, most guides were busy with their clients. In addition, the guides' association ruled that nobody could carry a load of more than fifteen kilos, which meant no large beams could be used. Nevertheless, the first hut, measuring five by four by three metres high, was erected inside two months and was ready for use by the end of July, 1890. Part of this was the first refuge. Later on the building was considerably enlarged.

A few days after the inauguration of the Vallot Observatory it was visited by Dr Jules Janssen, President of the French Academy of Sciences and Director of the astrophysical laboratory at Meudon, near Paris. Janssen was sixty-six years old, a strong-willed individual who had undertaken several important expeditions overseas, mainly in connection with eclipses and spectroscopic work. At the Vallot Observatory the weather gave him a fairly rough time, but he did manage to ascend Mont Blanc and came away convinced that the pure air met with at high altitude had distinct advantages for astrophysical observations. He determined to build his own observatory on the mountain – higher than Vallot's.

It was totally unnecessary; the observatory which Vallot had built could do anything that was required, but Janssen seems to have been jealous of Vallot's success and determined to go one better: the new observatory was to be built on the very summit of Mont Blanc. And as a person of considerable standing in the scientific world he had no problems in raising the necessary funds from his friends in Paris.

But outside his own rather rarefied social circle, his scheme was met with total incredulity, especially by anyone with mountaineering experience. It was pointed out to him that there are no rocks on the summit of Mont Blanc and it is not possible to build firm foundations in snow. Janssen was unperturbed. He explained to his critics that rock ridges support the mountain and must meet somewhere beneath the snow: all you had to do was dig deep enough. He sought the advice of a leading engineer, Alexandre Eiffel, who had just completed his eponymous tower in Paris. Eiffel not only guaranteed to build an observatory on the summit of Mont Blanc if rock could be found within fifteen metres of the surface but also to bear the cost of the initial exploration himself. He set the famous Swiss surveyor, M. X. Imfeld, to work on the project.

During the summer of 1891 Imfeld drove a tunnel twenty-nine metres long into the summit cap of Mont Blanc at a depth of fifteen metres. The only kind of stone he came across was a prune stone which must have been dropped by a climber on the summit many years earlier! Nor did the work go smoothly; there were storms and strikes and occasionally more serious accidents like that of August 21 when five workmen descended to the Grands Mulets for provisions, accompanied by a climber and his guide who also happened to be descending. They had reached the Petit Plateau when there was a loud bang as an ice-avalanche broke loose from the Dôme du Goûter and came bounding down at them. The tourist and guide were killed; the workmen escaped with slight bruises.

Then there was the strange case of Dr Jacottet, a medical man of Chamonix, who had twice tried to climb Mont Blanc and failed. He now persuaded Imfeld to take him up to the Vallot Hut for a few days from where, if conditions were right, he would climb the mountain. In return he offered his medical services free to the workmen.

They set out on August 28 and on September 1, the good doctor managed to reach the summit. He could hardly have chosen a less propitious moment, for suddenly several men were struck with mountain sickness and had to descend. Next day Jacottet himself fell ill. Imfeld's diary tells what happened: 'Dr Jacottet unwell (inflammation of the lungs and brain), and I remained at the Observatory to look after him . . . About 4 pm the condition of Dr Jacottet got worse (delirium). At 5.30 pm he lost consciousness, and he died in the course of the night, at 2.30 am.'

There is little doubt that what Imfeld is describing is a classic case of advanced mountain sickness where water accumulates on the lungs and brain (pulmonary and cerebral oedema). The swift onset of death is not unusual in such cases and the only known cure is to lose altitude as rapidly as possible. Possibly the doctor had had preliminary symptoms such as headache, but he can't have suspected mountain sickness for he had just sent several men down the mountain for precisely this cause.

Mountain sickness is no respecter of persons; it strikes indiscriminately at young and old, fit and unfit, men and women. A certain degree of adaptation can be got by gradual acclimatisation and some people are scarcely affected at all. The 4000-metre peaks of the Alps are just about the lowest limit at which the affliction can be expected, so Mont Blanc is the prime candidate, but there doesn't seem to be any evidence that it is common except in its milder forms, such as headache and loss of appetite. Of course, most people go down immediately they have climbed the mountain and so descend below the danger zone. But on the other hand Tyndall, Vallot and Imfeld's workmen, though they stayed at altitude, were habitual mountaineers and should have been acclimatised. It is all very curious.

At the end of the season Imfeld retired from the project but Janssen refused to abandon it. The work continued, no rock was discovered, so the observatory was built on the snow. Janssen should have remembered the prune stone and how it had sunk. It was all quite useless, of course; the place never functioned properly though Janssen himself twice visited it, drawn up the mountain on a sledge. The death of its originator in 1907 brought the work to an end and two years later the observatory was demolished. The wood was chopped up and used for heating the Vallot Hut.

The name of the Vallot family continued to be associated with Mont Blanc long after that observatory was completed. Joseph, with his brother Henri Vallot, began the compilation of a new map of the region on a scale of 1:20,000 and though Joseph died in 1925 before it was issued, the *Carte Vallot* was for many years the map used by climbers on their expeditions. Later there came a series of guidebooks, the *Guide Vallot*, describing all the climbs in the Mont Blanc range. It is the climbers' bible, updated at each new edition.

In August 1892, Vallot was at his observatory when:

Towards evening a cry of joy was heard outside, and all hands were outstretched to welcome Emile Rey. He was followed by a traveller of ripe age, stoutish, of rugged aspect; the iron crampons on his feet reminded me vaguely of a crocodile's jaws, and contributed somewhat to give him *un air rébarbatif.*

The stranger was Paul Güssfeldt, a German scientist and Privy Councillor to Kaiser Wilhem II, a man of great determination and strength in the mountains, even then, when he was fifty-two years old. He was a big solid man who did big solid climbs, not innovative as Mummery was because he always climbed with the best of guides, doing long routes on big mountains. Nevertheless, some of these were very impressive and when Vallot met him he and Rey had just made an ascent by the Brenva Glacier following a route made in 1881 by Gruber and Rey to the Col de la Brenva – and seemingly not done again until Walter Bonatti soloed it in 1961! In the previous year he and Rey had made the first winter ascent of the Grandes Jorasses and in the following year, 1893, when Güssfeldt was fifty-three, they made the first ascent of the Peuterey Ridge.

Of all the ridges on Mont Blanc, the Peuterey is undoubtedly the most majestic. In its entirety it begins with the savage looking Aiguille Noire, then comes a deep gap with the spiky looking Dames Anglaises followed by the majestic Aiguille Blanche which descends then to the Col Peuterey and the final ridge up to Mont Blanc de Courmayeur. The complete ridge was not done until 1935 and is a major undertaking even today. Güssfeldt's route started with the Aiguille Blanche – though as a point of interest he did the Aiguille Noire separately a few days before.

He had with him two first-rate guides, Emile Rey and a man from Eastern Switzerland, Christian Klucker, who was every bit Rey's equal both in skill and intelligence. Four porters accompanied them to their first bivouac and, after some persuasion – the Aiguille Blanche was dreaded by most guides and porters – one of these also accompanied the party for the rest of the trip. Güssfeldt's luck was working overtime, for the porter was César Ollier, who later turned out to be a first-class guide in his own right. So the party was immensely strong.

They approached the Aiguille Blanche from the east, across the Brenva Glacier. When Rey had made the first ascent of the peak, eight years earlier, he and his companions had done so from the west side by a very circuitous route and returned the same way. For a traverse a new approach was necessary, although they all knew that the east side of the Aiguille Blanche was subject to heavy stonefall. Nevertheless, the going proved easy enough and they managed to bivouac for the night high on the slopes of the mountain where a rocky rib gave them protection from anything that might fall during the night. Rey had wanted to halt lower down, but Klucker would have none of it, pointing out how much safer the upper bivouac site would be. As the porters prepared the site for a bivouac, Rey cooked the supper and Klucker went on ahead to scout out the route for next morning. Güssfeldt, as befits a high German official, merely satisfied himself that everything was being done that should be done.

Next day they were away at 4.30 am, having persuaded Ollier to join them. Their route was a diagonal one across the face of the peak and led them across various gullies, sometimes scree-filled, sometimes icy and always potential death traps. Now and then they could hear the ominous whine of a falling stone. These grew more frequent as the sun made its appearance, shedding its warming rays on the ice-bound debris. 'It began to get lively above our heads,' said Güssfeldt, '. . . we decided to cross towards the left over two steep snow gullies, but before we had advanced a hundred steps we were driven back by falling stones.'

Fortunately they were able to reach a rock rib which led them to the final snow cap and so to the summit; an exquisitely delicate little point. The time was eleven am. It was the second ascent of the mountain.

It took them more than two hours to descend the ridge to the Col de Peuterey, then they began the climb up the opposite ridge towards Mont Blanc de Courmayeur. The afternoon was extremely hot and by three pm they had had enough. A bivouac was inevitable in any case and this seemed as good a place as any.

In the late afternoon clouds began boiling up from the valley giving some concern over the weather prospects, but with evening the clouds evaporated, leaving a clear, still starry night. The four climbers were perched on a narrow ledge at over 4250 metres, overhanging an unimaginable void.

'All is silence about us,' wrote Güssfeldt. 'Silently and surely, too, the cold invades us.' They all suffered greatly from the intense cold. Sleep was impossible and Rey tried to keep up their spirits by singing the 'Lisette' of Béranger, which had been their battle-cry since the winter ascent of the Grandes Jorasses. For thirteen hours they remained on this ledge, for the climbing was too difficult to begin until daylight. As dawn rose they partook of a meagre breakfast – Güssfeldt's was a raw egg which was so cold it had become granulated – and drank a bottle of champagne to dispel the numbing effects of the cold night.

When they did at last start again, stiff and cramped, they discovered that the ridge was hard ice requiring a good deal of step cutting. They made little more than 200 metres in two hours and a half and in desperation sought relief by climbing some adjacent rocks, but the rocks were poor, ice glazed and altogether unpleasant, which caused them to waste some four hours trying to extricate themselves again. But eventually, at 12.55 pm they reached the top of Mont Blanc de Courmayeur and an hour later, the summit of Mont Blanc.

Two English climbers, A. M. Marshall and T. L. Kesteven, who were on the summit that day watched the party wearily approaching, 'Güssfeldt himself being completely done up', according to Kesteven. From Emile Rey they learned that they had had nothing proper to eat for seventeen hours, so the Englishmen immediately offered Güssfeldt all their own provisions which were gratefully accepted. 'We had nothing to do but to run down to Chamonix,' Kesteven later explained.

That night Güssfeldt and his companions spent the night in the workmen's hut near the Rochers Rouges inhabited by the men who were working on Janssen's observatory. The small cabin was crowded with fourteen bodies and the German scientist had 'a most dreadful night' – one senses that he much preferred the cold bivouac of the previous night.

One can only imagine that it was intellectual curiosity regarding Janssen's work which directed Güssfeldt to the Rochers Rouges rather than the more comfortable Vallot Hut, especially as next day he descended to the Grand Plateau, climbed from there the Dôme du Goûter and descended to the Dôme Glacier, thus returning to the Val Veni and Courmayeur. The whole expedition, from start to finish, lasted eighty-eight hours. It cost Güssfeldt about sixty pounds, which was quite a sum in those days.

A few years later Paul Preuss made a different start to the traverse of the Aiguille Blanche, one less prone to stonefall: it improves the route without adding to the difficulty, which was in any case never excessive. J. P. Farrar, who repeated it a fortnight after Güssfeldt, said of it, 'There is no reason why it should not be repeated, but the members of the party had *better* be very fit, and the weather *ought* to be without reproach.' It was a serious, classic climb in the grand manner.

Klucker, perhaps piqued at being only second guide to Rey, rarely referred to the climb. He didn't care for Dr Güssfeldt, whom he thought was a poor climber and he once told Farrar, with whom he climbed quite regularly, that he and Farrar could have done the ridge in a day.

It was Rey's last great climb. He was the finest of the Italian guides, combining strength and intelligence. 'I've always been lucky,' he once remarked. Yet he was fully aware of his powers and had supreme faith in his own ability. Two years after the Peuterey climb he was descending a steep ice slope on Mont Maudit, cutting steps and held on a very tight rope by his employer. Rey told him to slacken the rope a little. 'It isn't necessary, monsieur,' he explained in his usual self-confident manner. 'I never slip.'

Three days later, descending unroped on some easy rocks below the Aiguille du Géant, Emile Rey fell to his death.

Guideless climbing continued to grow in popularity, especially amongst continentals who took to heart the philosophy which Mummery had stated in his book *My Climbs in the Alps and Caucasus*, published shortly before his death in 1895. In it he poured scorn on climbers who were content to follow guides along well-beaten paths, urging that real climbers were those who faced the unknown armed only with their skills. To John Ruskin's famous taunt that climbers treated mountains as greased poles he asked what was wrong with climbing poles? Many young climbers agreed.

In the Eastern Alps the movement was already strong, but in France it didn't really get under way until about 1907 when the de Lépiney brothers, Jacques and Tom, gathered about them a group of outstanding climbers like Le Bec, Bregeault and Alice Damesme. In 1914 they formed the Groupe des Rochassiers which in 1919, during a bivouac on the Peuterey Ridge, became the Groupe de Haute Montagne (GHM); an association restricted to the very best alpinists, dedicated to high standard climbing.

Teams from the Eastern Alps were spreading westwards, too. In 1900 Heinrich Pfannl, with T. Maischburger and F. Zimmer, climbed a new route on the Aiguille du Géant by the North Ridge and North-West Face, which required none of the artificial aids used on the original route – and remains today the only 'free' route on the peak. As such it would certainly have found favour with another Eastern climber, Dr Paul Preuss, who was an advocate of the freest possible climbing, often preferring to solo the most difficult routes. His introduction to the Western Alps, in 1912, was traumatic.

On the evening of August 12 Paul Preuss arrived at the recently constructed Gamba Hut which stood on the easy lower slopes of the Innominata Ridge, to find that it was occupied by an English party and their Swiss guides. Preuss would know he was in distinguished company, for Geoffrey Winthrop Young, Dr H. O. Jones and the guide Josef Knubel were the conquerors of the East Face of the Grépon the previous year, one of the long-standing problems of the Mont Blanc range. With them was Mrs Jones and a second guide, Julius Truffer. That day the four men had made the first ascent of the most northerly of the spiky needles called the Dames Anglaises, to which Young gave the name l'Isolée, because it was rather separate from the others.

Next day Young and Knubel descended to Courmayeur in a torrential downpour, but the others stayed at the hut, hoping that better weather might give an opportunity for a short climb. Preuss discovered that Dr and Mrs Jones were highly qualified scientists, as he himself was – and they were on their honeymoon.

On Thursday, August 15, the weather had cleared sufficiently to allow them to attempt an adjacent minor peak, Mont Rouge de Peuterey (2941m), by a new route which was not expected to be difficult. From the Gamba Hut their way led down onto the lower part of the Frêney Glacier, where Truffer and the two Jones roped up. Preuss wasn't happy about the order of the rope. He thought that Jones should go second after Truffer and Mrs Jones last, as the weakest member of the party, but Jones stuck to the theory that in a rope of three the weakest member goes in the middle. As he pointed out, there might be a traverse involved when patently the person in the middle of the rope is best protected. In any case, Muriel Jones was a reasonably competent climber. She had led all-women ropes over the Pinnacle Ridge in Skye and the Idwal Slabs in Wales.

They were tackling the North-North-West Ridge of the peak and the climbing turned out to be complicated. According to Preuss, the difficulty was similar to that of the Funffingerspitze in the Dolomites. They climbed mostly on the crest of the ridge but at one point they were forced to move out onto the Frêney side, where Preuss, who was racing ahead, had climbed a two-metre chimney and sat on top waiting for the others. Truffer climbed the chimney but as he pulled up on the final hold it suddenly broke away and he fell over backwards. He catapulted out into space, missing Mrs Jones who was directly below him at the foot of the chimney, but landing on her husband who was a few steps behind. Jones was knocked from his holds and he in turn plucked his wife from hers. Without a sound, the three bodies spiralled through the air to land sickeningly on the Frêney Glacier, three hundred metres below. Paul Preuss, alone and badly shaken, made his way down to Courmayeur to raise the alarm.

The accident provoked a Third Leader from *The Times* on the subject of mountain accidents, but not nearly so thunderous as that of fifty years earlier after the Matterhorn tragedy. Mountain accidents were becoming more common; accepted, if not understood. At the funeral in Courmayeur there was a gathering of the leading British climbers: Young, Eckenstein, Mallory, Pope and Reade.

When the North-North-West Ridge of Mont Rouge was eventually climbed, in 1925, it turned out to be quite difficult.

In the year following the accident Preuss returned to the south side of Mont Blanc where he climbed the Pointe Gamba and the Punta Innominata with Ugo di Vallepiana and then, late in August, with Carl Prochownick and Count Aldo Bonacossa made the first complete traverse of the Aiguille Blanche de Peuterey from the Dames Anglaises col to the Col Peuterey.

Preuss was fascinated by the idea of traversing the entire Peuterey Ridge from the Aiguille Noire to the summit of Mont Blanc. The challenge was starkly obvious and the idea must have occurred to many climbers before him, only to be dismissed as an impossible dream. The length of such an expedition would be prodigious; the difficulties extreme. But 'impossible' was not a word Preuss understood and he made plans for the grand traverse which he hoped to undertake the following summer, 1914.

It was not to be. In the autumn of 1913 Paul Preuss was killed attempting to solo the North Ridge of the Mandlwand in the Eastern Alps. His erstwhile companions had refused to accompany him; it was, they said, impossible.

If during these years guideless climbing was beginning to make its mark, there were still many climbers who sometimes climbed with guides and sometimes without. Amongst these were Giuseppe F. and Giovanni Battista Gugliermina, two Italian brothers from the Val Sesia who made a number of notable routes on Mont Blanc. They were not unlike their English contemporaries, the Abraham brothers of Keswick, in that both pairs lugged a heavy plate camera round the mountains with them and both seemed to have a sense of fun about their adventures. Those of the Italians, however, were on an altogether grander scale: Giovanni Battista with the guide Joseph Brocherel made the first ascent of the Brouillard Ridge in 1901 and both brothers, with their friends Ettore Canzio and Giuseppe Lampugnani made the first ascent of the Nant Blanc Face of the Aiguille Verte, guideless, in 1904. The Pointe Gugliermina, a rock tower on the south ridge of the Aiguille Blanche, is named in their honour and it was climbed for the first time by Giovanni Battista and Francesco Ravelli in 1914. Both brothers lived to be nearly ninety and Giovanni Battista made his last first ascent at the age of eighty!

It is perhaps fitting though that this long Indian summer before the First World War should see the last of the great guided partnerships – that combination of talents which had been the very foundation of alpinism. After the war things were never quite the same again, in mountaineering as in much else, and though there were great guides and great climbs done with guides, the scene was very different and the classic mould was broken. Who needed a partner in the jazz age?

But before the storm broke there were some very strong teams in the field, like the Mayer brothers who climbed with the great Dolomite guide, Angelo Dibona. Guido Mayer was responsible for the classic Mayer-Dibona route on the Requin in 1913; a very accessible and consequently very popular climb, just above the Requin Hut.

The premier guide in Chamonix at this period was Joseph Ravanel, called Ravanel le Rouge because of his red hair. Like many guides, he came up through a hard school. When he was fourteen his father died, leaving him as chief breadwinner for a family of nine children. Perhaps it was the memory of this early hardship which drove him to the top of his profession, for he was not, in the technical sense, a polished climber – 'Dashing,' was how the English climber C. F. Meade once described him. 'He was a bold and omnivorous rock climber . . . not a graceful performer, however, for he fought his way up his mountains by force, and his courage was even greater than his skill.' He had a ready wit and a social ease which allowed him to be at home even in the most illustrious company. Among his clients was King Albert of the Belgians.

Ravanel's speciality was the rocky aiguilles of his home district – he climbed the Grépon fifty-seven times – and amongst his first ascents can be counted those of the Aiguilles Carrée, Fou, Ravanel, Mummery, Pélerins, and Peigne; almost all of them popular climbs today. He also discovered the Passage en Z between the Grand and Petit Drus, which is the key to the modern traverse of these peaks. Many of Ravanel's best climbs were done with Emile Fontaine, one of the best climbers of the day but a very modest man who refused to have his own name attached to any of the many pinnacles he and Ravanel climbed together. In 1902 they made the first ascent of a very fine pinnacle on the South-East Ridge of les Courtes and when they reached the top Ravanel found there a small pool of water. Discovering such a 'fontaine', said Ravanel with sly logic, made the naming of the peak obvious – but Fontaine would have none of it and called the peak Ravanel instead. In the following year they climbed the twin peak of the Aiguille Ravanel and the guide once again urged that it be called Fontaine, but Fontaine shook his head. 'The man who has done most for climbing in these mountains has never been adequately commemorated,' he said. And so it became Aiguille Mummery.

Though French, German and Italian parties were beginning to make their mark in the Mont Blanc range, for a short time at least the ascendancy was still with the British. Two very strong partnerships came to the fore: V. J. E. Ryan with the Valais guides Franz and Josef Lochmatter, and Geoffrey Winthrop Young with Josef Knubel, who was also from the Valais. For some of their greatest climbs these men combined their talents, though they seldom climbed together in the Mont Blanc area.

Ryan was an Irishman, a climber whose appearances were spasmodic like some erratic comet shining brilliantly in the Alpine firmament for an hour or two then vanishing, only to reappear with equal brilliance a few years later. He seems to have been a man of fits and moods who drove his guides remorselessly, never smiled and was generally disliked. Small wonder that when he applied for membership of the Alpine Club in 1906, he was promptly blackballed although, like Mummery with whom he shares the distinction, his record of climbs was outstanding.

In fact, amongst his many climbs of the previous season there were repeats of Mummery's routes on the West Face of the Plan and the Charpoua Face of the Verte; the first time anyone had dared repeat them – almost a quarter of a century later in the case of the Verte. In that same year, too, he climbed the Grépon from the Mer de Glace, thus solving one of the long-standing problems of the area, though his route was later to be eclipsed by an even finer one by Young.

Here indeed was great talent, but Ryan was matched by his guides, the Lochmatter brothers and especially Franz, who always took the lead when the going got tough. The Lochmatters came from a family of guides, allied to the Pollingers and the Knubels, all from the village of St Niklaus in Valais. Their father, J.-M. Lochmatter, had been killed on the Dent Blanche in 1882 with his eldest son Alexander, but the four remaining sons all became outstanding guides. Their father had wisely seen that they had a good education and this undoubtedly helped, for the role of the guide was changing to that of guide-companion and horizons were being widened for the best guides. Franz led five expeditions to the Himalaya.

He was a tall man with long arms and legs and fingers 'like potential steel hooks'. He climbed with graceful simian movements, his body seeming to adapt itself to the rock.

In 1906 Ryan and his guides put up two of the district's classic rock climbs: the North-West Ridge of the Aiguille de Blaitière and the east ridge of the Aiguille du Plan, known ever since as the Ryan-Lochmatter Route. It was on this latter climb that the Lochmatters adopted a daring tactic to overcome an overhang. The ledge on which they were standing was too narrow and precarious to allow the usual shoulder tactics, where one man climbs onto the other's shoulders to reach higher holds, so they traversed across the rock to a broader ledge. There Franz climbed onto his brother's shoulders. Josef gripped Franz's ankles and together they traversed back again, Josef providing the footholds and Franz the handholds, until they reached the place where Franz could continue his upwards progress!

It was Ryan's greatest year and though he returned to the Alps from time to time, and with the Lochmatters did some more splendid climbs, he gradually lost interest in the sport and even became hostile to it.

Geoffrey Winthrop Young was a very different character

altogether: a flamboyant personality with perhaps a hint of the poseur about him. According to Arnold Lunn, Young was to the decade before the War what Whymper had been to the Golden Age or Mummery to the age which followed, and as with them his fame owed as much to his books as his climbs. Certainly nobody described their climbs more elegantly than Young, but his books show none of the fiery zeal which was Whymper's or the quantum leaps of Mummery. Nevertheless, his climbs were outstanding.

Young was the second son of Sir George Young, one of the Alpine pioneers who had met with an accident when descending Mont Blanc with his two brothers in 1866. Bulkeley Young was killed and since the party was unguided, Sir George felt himself to be responsible for his brother's death. He not only gave up climbing but the subject of mountaineering was banned from the Young household. Perhaps he should have recognised that nothing is more tempting to an adventurous lad than forbidden fruit. 'Will I ever see the Alps?' young Geoffrey scribbled in his school hymnal.

He not only saw the Alps, but played a large part in their story. Few men have been so utterly dedicated to mountaineering, whether on his beloved Welsh crags or in the Alps, even though he lost a leg in the war when serving as an ambulance driver. He was the driving force behind the foundation of the British Mountaineering Council, the governing body of the sport in Britain, and he stimulated home climbing clubs with a fervour similar to that of Cecil Slingsby, whose daughter he married.

He was immensely strong and fast so that despite some long expeditions he was never obliged to spend a night out in a forced bivouac. On one occasion he and Josef Knubel traversed the Charmoz, Grépon and Blaitière in a single day, because their ridges made a geometric pattern which pleased him!

Young was well matched with his guide, little Josef Knubel, whom he once described as having a, 'neat, small framework of steel and whalebone that serves him for a body'. He smoked strong, black, Swiss cheroots interminably, even when climbing and the Swiss climber, Alfred Zurcher, tells how once he was reduced to a fit of coughing by Knubel's acrid tobacco smoke: 'Josef gave me a pitying smile, but quietly stubbed out his Montheyer and just lengthened his stride a little.'

117

Knubel was a religious man who attended Mass before and after each climb and whose strongest expletive was 'Holy smoke!' He once upbraided Zurcher for swearing: 'I don't suppose our Master up there will be taking much pleasure from the conversation of my master down here,' he said.

Some of his expeditions were prodigious: double traverses of Mont Blanc and the Weisshorn, first complete traverse of the Grandes Jorasses, the Lauper Route on the Eiger and many more. He climbed all the 4000-metre peaks in the Alps. He was also a keen winter climber and, after Arnold Lunn gave him a pair of skis, he became a pioneering ski guide.

Young and Knubel had their greatest season in 1911. H. O. Jones was with them throughout and they were joined by others from time to time as they stormed their way up some of the last great problems of the district. They began by an ascent of the Brouillard Ridge using a new approach from the Col Emile Rey which was much more logical than the Gugliermina route of ten years earlier. The rock was just as rotten, however, and the Brouillard Ridge was never destined to gain the popularity of the great Peuterey Ridge nearby. The expedition did have one small landmark, however; they were accompanied by Dr Karl Blodig, a Swiss dentist who was a noted mountaineer. As the party attained the summit of Pointe Louis Amédée (4460m) on the ridge, Blodig became the first man to have climbed all the 4000-metre peaks then known in the Alps.

From there they turned their attention to the Grandes Jorasses, a coxcomb of a mountain lying east to west along the frontier between France and Italy. Since its ascent by Whymper and Walker in pioneering days various routes had been made up the Italian face, but very little of consequence. The impressive North Face had not been touched at all, though Young and Knubel had looked closely at the long spur descending from the Pointe Croz before deciding it was impossible. What was rapidly becoming apparent to the new breed of alpinists was that apart from the ordinary ways up it was a very difficult mountain indeed. Even the main ridges, east and west, were proving extraordinarily stubborn.

These were the ridges which Young decided to tackle in 1911, beginning with the eastern one, which reared up sharply from the Col des Hirondelles. It had been tried previously, but nobody had managed to pass a difficult notch in the ridge, quite near the start, and Young fared no better. He decided instead that he would begin at the top and *descend* the ridge, so on August 11, with Jones, Knubel and a second guide, Laurent Croux, they climbed the usual route to the summit and made their way carefully down the ridge which they found much trickier than they had expected. At the final notch they were forced to abseil, the rock being too steep to climb down. It was an exciting expedition, and some small recompense for initial disappointments. Nor were they the last to be disappointed on this ridge: from the first attempt in 1881 until success by a strong Italian party in 1927, there were at least thirty-six attempts.

Three days later Young, Jones and Knubel attempted the west ridge. This is double the length of the Hirondelles Ridge but a totally different piece of architecture. From the Col des Grandes Jorasses it rises steeply to a tower, now called the Pointe Young (3996m), then in a series of swooping arcs it leaps from pinnacle to pinnacle along the frontier ridge – the Pointe Marguerite (4065m), Pointe Hélène (4045m), Pointe Croz (4110m), Pointe Whymper (4184m), and finally Pointe Walker (4208m). This sounds a formidable undertaking, but in fact the only real difficulty lies between the first two pinnacles. Pointe Young had been reached before its namesake ever trod its summit, by Ryan and the Lochmatters, but they had been unable to force the ridge beyond.

Young's party met with complete success. The climbing was difficult – including a thirty-metre hand traverse, which is the climber's way of saying that though there were handholds there were no footholds, so the only way to progress is in the manner of our Darwinian ancestors. In two hours they were across the gap and had reached Pointe Marguerite; in a further hour and three-quarters they were on Pointe Whymper, the second summit of the Grandes Jorasses. Like Whymper himself they went no further, indeed, Jones didn't even bother to go to the Pointe Whymper but turned directly down the mountain along the usual way off. Perhaps in its own small way this indicates how the feelings of climbers were changing – the summit was no longer of great consequence; it was the route that mattered.

A few days later the same party were joined by Ralph Todhunter and the guide Henri Brocherel in the climb which more than any other was to mark the climax of the long Indian summer of pre-war climbing, the Mer de Glace Face of the Grépon. It was a long-standing challenge where some of the best had tried and failed; a test piece whose symbolism was as important as the route itself.

The newcomer to Young's party, Ralph Todhunter was, at forty-four, considerably older than the others and a somewhat reticent character; an accusation that could hardly be levelled at the rest of the party. Like them, though, he had considerable Alpine experience at the highest standards and was proficient on Welsh rock, being one of the first to climb on the formidable crag of Clogwyn Du'r Arddu.

They bivouacked below the mountain's East Face and on August 19, shortly after three am, climbed up the modest Trélaporte Glacier which fringes the rocks. After a little trouble with the bergschrund, they started to climb towards a prominent feature known as the Tour Rouge. The granite was rough and solid, the holds sound and there was no stone fall. As crack and chimney followed each other in entertaining fashion, they scrambled up towards the Red Tower, which was the limit of Mummery's exploration thirty years before. They were roped up with Knubel leading, followed by Brocherel, then Young, Jones and Todhunter. It peeved Jones to find Todhunter constantly at his heels, sauntering up the steep rock with the rope casually coiled in his white gloved hands, 'in order to save time'. He felt he was being chased up the cliff by a pair of white gloves (an affectation of Todhunter's), for no sooner would he reach a stance, than white fingers would appear over the edge of the rock.

Soon they were past the Tour Rouge and climbing a rib up the centre of the face. For over ninety metres it led them towards the pinnacled ridge high above their heads, but then, just as things seemed to be going so well, it played them false and they found themselves lost on holdless slabs. It was Young who found the key to the problem: he moved left across a difficult gully, where they found a continuation line which took them to a comfortable triangular ledge they christened the Niche des Amis.

Pitch followed pitch. Jones later described the climbing as, 'always difficult, usually exceedingly difficult, twice verging on the impossible, but – it was undoubtedly superb!' The first occasion on which it verged on the impossible was when they reached the foot of a deep chimney, interrupted by an overhang. Knubel swarmed over the bulge followed by the larger Brocherel who took some time to grunt his way up. They disappeared from the view of their companions who were stationed one above the other on minute holds part way up the chimney. They were there for some time while, unseen from below, Knubel was struggling desperately with bulging rock. First he had to climb onto Brocherel's shoulders then climb up, hooking his ice axe into nicks in the rock in a method peculiar to himself and his friend Franz Lochmatter which they called 'the axe cling'. Needless to say, the others found the pitch extremely difficult. As Jones remarked, even the white gloves of Todhunter didn't follow with their usual swiftness.

At last they reached the foot of the final pinnacle of the Grépon and the finest pitch of the climb. They could have avoided it; they could have moved round to the ordinary way up, which was only a few feet away, but they were all agreed that such a superb climb should have its own independent finish. And there was one staring them in the face; a twenty-metre crack of intimidating aspect.

Knubel once more climbed onto Brocherel's shoulders, for the start of the crack was too smooth to begin without aid. There still seemed no holds, so he tried hooking his axe in and scrabbling up, but this proved useless. Suddenly, to everyone's amazement, Knubel leaned out from the rock and with a mighty blow jammed the shaft of his axe deep into the crack above his head, so that it stuck out like a barber's pole. With superb audacity he then swung on the axe like a gymnast on a bar and pulled himself up until he could stand on it and grip the rock above. The Mer de Glace face was conquered at last.

The Knubel Crack on the Grépon was probably the hardest single pitch of any climb in the Western Alps in its day.

The long Victorian summer had outlasted the Queen herself and her son Edward too. But in 1914 it came to a sudden, bloody, end.

7 'In this profession you must learn how to suffer!'

The machine guns of the Somme not only wiped out a youthful generation, but brought an end to a long established social order throughout Europe. In some places the effect was immediate and violent, in other more ordered societies it was a gradual transition which wasn't completed until after the Second World War.

There were well-known mountaineers on both sides who died in the war – Herford, Dülfer, Innerkofler and others. Who knows whether they had reached their full potential, or what their contributions to the sport might have been had they lived? One effect was noticeable; British climbers no longer dominated the Alpine scene. In Britain Alpine climbing remained a sport for the well-to-do middle classes, partly because they were the ones who could most readily afford the expense of visiting the Alps and partly because there was as yet no large home-based mountaineering background to which the ordinary man and woman could relate. Climbing in Britain was still small beer and the few clubs which existed were very much middle-class preserves.

On the Continent it was different. If you were out of work, with time on your hands, all you needed to get to the Alps was some bread and cheese and a second-hand bicycle. The Continental clubs had always been mass movements, cheap to join and totally classless. The ground was fertile for widespread growth.

Most of this growth was in guideless climbing simply because many of the new participants could not afford to employ a guide. Some of them even became guides themselves, though they were born far away from the mountains in Paris or Stuttgart or wherever, which was a radical departure from the long established guiding 'families' of the Alpine villages like the Lochmatters, the Charlets, the Taugwalders and others. Many chose to climb without guides because they preferred it that way, disciples of Mummery. As far as ability was concerned, there was nothing to choose between the best amateurs and the best guides, though as the years went on the former began to outweigh the latter in sheer numbers.

In 1911 a French instructional book, *Carnet de l'Alpiniste*, was advising climbers to carry a second silk shirt, a tie, slippers, hairbrush, barometer and thermometer. It also advised that a party coming to a route which somebody else had reached first should gracefully retire and seek another one. Ten years later anyone quoting from the book could be sure of raising ribald laughter. The new creed was to travel light and travel fast, and if you caught up with a party on a climb, then you climbed past them.

There were a lot more people climbing and if you believe the dictum that more means worse, there were probably a lot more climbing badly. But there were also more climbing at the top level than there had been – so many, in fact, that from here on only the most interesting or important climbs can be described and probably not all of those. The story of Mont Blanc between the wars is dominated by the campaigns against various 'last great problems' like the South Ridge of the Noire, the Charmoz North Face, the Brenva climbs and, of course, the North Face of the Grandes Jorasses, but it should be remembered that there were many other fine climbs done too; 'one-offs', like the splendidly difficult rock climbs done on the south side of Mont Blanc by Gabriele Boccalatte and Nina Pietrasanta.

Membership of the élite Groupe de Haute Montagne was based on a points scale, which was itself based on the guides' charges for various routes; for example, a first-class climb, costing 100 francs, rated 100 points if done with a guide or 200 if done guideless. An 'exceptional route' such as the traverse of the Drus or traverse of the Grépon rated 150 or 300 points. For active membership 1000 points were needed, at least three first-class expeditions included, and this had to be topped up with 200 points per year. Members also had to be members of the French Alpine Club and finally, they had to be approved by the Committee. There were twenty-nine members initially, including two women, Bailly Lereins and Alice Damesme.

They were the spiritual heirs to Mummery and it was fitting that three leading members, Jacques Lagarde, Jacques de Lépiney

and Henry Ségogne should make the first ascent of the North
Face of the Plan in 1924, the face which had defeated Mummery
thirty-two years earlier. In that same year Lagarde and de
Ségogne, with Jacques de Lépiney's brother, Tom, made the
second ascent of the notorious Cordier Couloir, forty-eight years
after Middlemore and Jaun's brave lead.

Perhaps because there were so many more people climbing and doing so at higher standards, elegance, style and
times began to assume proportions they had never had
before. It wasn't enough to do a climb; it had to be done well
and since the easiest way to judge this was by the time taken,
time was used as a measure of competence. This was fine up to
a point – sometimes speed is essential to get the best out
of snow conditions – but it became something of a fetish,
especially amongst guides, who would rip off climbs at a rate
of knots which left their clients utterly shattered by the end of
the day.

Claire Eliane Engel, the mountain historian, tells how she was
once crossing the séracs on the Géant Glacier when the great
guide Armand Charlet came hurtling past, with the English
climber Wilf Noyce. 'They were almost running,' she com-
ments, adding that it was more like dancing than the uphill toil
one expects on a glacier. This was all very well for someone like
Noyce, who was no slouch himself when it came to mountain
travel, but too many guides adopted the same method with
clients who were far less able. Nor has it entirely died out.

Charlet was undoubtedly the leading Chamonix guide of the
period with many fine climbs to his credit including the Nant
Blanc face of the Verte, his favourite mountain, which he did
with Dimitri Platanov in 1935. He was an austere man, teetotaler
and non-smoker, who could be abrasive with his clients.
'Armand was far from being an easy person to climb or deal
with,' records Douglas Busk, who knew him well. 'He was no
"ladies' guide" in the Swiss tradition.'

His speed in the mountains was phenomenal: the Peuterey
Ridge in ten hours, from the valley; the old Brenva in four and a
half hours, from the Fourche Hut; the Grépon traverse and back
to Montenvers in seven and a half hours; the Drus traverse in
nine hours and, perhaps the most remarkable of all, the Mer de
Glace Face of the Grépon from Montenvers in four and a half

hours, and return to Montenvers in two hours! This latter was done with Wilf Noyce, incidentally.

But Charlet was also a traditionalist at a time when traditions were changing under increasing pressure from the 'hard men' of the Eastern Alps. He never used a piton and his model was Franz Lochmatter, the great Swiss guide of the immediate pre-war years. He was Mayor of his village, Argentière, for twenty years, and after the Second World War he became technical director of the École Nationale de Ski et d'Alpinisme at Chamonix, where guides from all over France came to obtain their diploma, and where they bounced between two lots of granite – the aiguilles and Armand Charlet. 'In this profession you must learn how to suffer,' he told them.

Charlet may not have been a ladies' man in the old sense but there was one woman climber of the period for whom he had great respect. Her name was Miriam O'Brien, a wealthy New Englander who had learned to climb in the White Mountains of New Hampshire and could afford to visit the Alps regularly, bringing her Buick car with her. She was a skilful climber, strong and resourceful; full of New England common sense. She could afford to climb with the very best guides like Charlet, Dibona and the Dimai brothers, yet often climbed guideless and on one memorable occasion, actually reversed roles with her guide to lead him on a traverse of the Grépon.

But perhaps Miriam O'Brien will be best remembered by her own sex as the innovator of guideless climbing in the Alps for what she called 'manless' ropes. In 1929 she and Winifred Marples climbed the Peigne and she traversed the Grépon with Alice Damesme. She was the spiritual heir to Lily Bristow.

In 1927, with the guides Alfred Couttet and Georges Cachat, she made the first ascent of the difficult Aiguille du Roc, which sticks out like a finger on the Mer de Glace side of the Grépon, and a few days later she and Margaret Helburn made the first women's ascent of Young's classic Mer de Glace Face. The guides on this occasion were Couttet – and Armand Charlet.

The following summer, 1928, Miriam O'Brien was back at Chamonix, this time with a fellow American, Robert Underhill, whom she subsequently married. Like his companion, Bob Underhill was a very fine climber, and when they found they had a few days to spare before a pre-arranged meeting with some friends, they sought out Armand Charlet and put to him a daring proposition – a traverse of the Aiguilles du Diable Ridge on Mont Blanc du Tacul.

The south-east ridge of Mont Blanc du Tacul is a lot shorter than the grand ridges which sweep down on the Italian side of Mont Blanc itself, but no less dramatic. It pokes out into the top-most corner of the Géant Glacier and terminates in a remarkable cluster of gigantic rock pinnacles, like stacked spear-heads. Most impressive of these is Le Grand Capucin, whose cock-eyed top like a monk's cowl was to act as a magnet to the next generation of climbers. As it climbs towards the peak, however, the ridge gathers itself together and shoots skywards in a series of five huge pinnacles which march along the crest – the Aiguilles du Diable. Each pinnacle has a name: going up the ridge they are Corne du Diable (4064m), Pointe Chaubert (4074m), Médiane (4097), Pointes Carmen (4019m) and finally, l'Isolée (4114m). Between the Chaubert and Médiane there is a very deep gap, or brèche, and similarly between Carmen and l'Isolée, but the most remarkable thing about this remarkable ridge is the consistent height of the pinnacles themselves – each is just over the 4000-metre mark. Since they are now considered to be individual summits they present something of a problem for anyone attempting to climb all the 4000-metre summits of the Alps: these are the most technically difficult of the lot.

The ridge was first explored in 1920, but it wasn't until 1923 that a strong party from the GHM, Jacques de Lépiney, Paul Chevalier and Henri Bregeault managed to climb the twin-peaked Carmen. Two years later l'Isolée was climbed by the pianist Emile Blanchet with Armand Charlet and Antoine Ravanel. It was the highest remaining unclimbed peak at the time and proved extremely difficult. The pinnacle was renamed Pointe Blanchet, after the fashion of the day, but for some reason the name never gained acceptance – perhaps because the original name described the pinnacle perfectly. Jean Chaubert fared better: with Charlet and Ravanel, he climbed his epony-mous pinnacle that same year and the Corne du Diable as well. Finally, in 1926, Blanchet and Chaubert joined forces and together with Charlet and the guide Jean Devouassoux they climbed Pointe Médiane. Blanchet summed it all up, 'Without offering any passages as difficult as those on l'Isolée, the

Médiane is more tiring . . . It is infinitely more difficult than the Drus, and the most dangerous of the five Aiguilles du Diable.'

So by 1926 all five had been climbed and Charlet had been involved in the ascent of four of them. All but the Médiane were quickly repeated and thus the position stood when Miriam O'Brien and Robert Underhill appeared on the scene in 1928. Two years earlier, in the GHM journal, Charlet had suggested that a traverse of all five pinnacles in one continuous expedition might be feasible and it was this that had attracted Miriam O'Brien, but both parties were cautious:

'How many do you want to do?' asked Charlet.
'As many as possible,' replied Miriam.
'We might do the three upper ones,' said the guide.

In fact, Charlet knew that this was exactly the party he had been waiting for, strong enough to follow him up the ridge over all the pinnacles, and Miriam O'Brien had no intention of doing anything less.

There was one slight problem. Charlet was already under engagement to a Scottish schoolmaster, Mr Burford, who was climbing in the area with a party of his pupils. As luck would have it he was a friend of Miriam's and he agreed to release Charlet – for one day!

As they all marched up the Géant Glacier next day to the Torino Hut – Charlet, Georges Cachat, a porter, O'Brien, Underhill, Burford and the schoolboys – the prospects for success did not look good. The weather was doubtful; black clouds hung over the Peuterey Ridge and that night, when they should have started at eleven pm, the weather was cloudy and warm, instead of clear and cold as they had hoped. But they only had one day, after which Charlet had to return to the school party who were going to amuse themselves on the Midi in his absence. So at one am on August 4, they decided to go for it fast, hoping the weather would improve.

The Diable Ridge is some two miles from the Torino Hut, across the top edge of the Géant Glacier. To reach its crest involves 450 metres of steep climbing, with a difficult berg-schrund to cross at the start, and all done in the hours of darkness. Charlet's party were on the crest three hours after leaving the hut.

The pinnacles followed in rapid succession, with flurries of snow urging the party on: Corne du Diable 5.10 am, Pointe Chaubert 5.45 am, Médiane 8.15 am, Pointe Carmen 9.50 am, l'Isolée 11.40 am – and the summit of Mont Blanc du Tacul 1.10 pm. Thus they did the entire ridge in some nine hours; including some of the most difficult rock-climbing done in the range at that time. Furthermore, they descended via the Col du Midi and the Géant Icefall to Montenvers by 7.30 pm, in nice time for dinner.

It was a remarkable *tour de force*, hailed at the time as the most difficult ridge climb in the Alps, though the crux, l'Isolée, was not as difficult as the Knubel Crack on the Grépon, according to Charlet. Perhaps more than anything it was a supreme demonstration of the traditional alpinism which Charlet represented; no pitons, no bivouacs, travel light and travel fast.

The ridge was repeated the following year by two Swiss climbers, André Roch and Jimmy Belaieff. Roch was one of the new breed of gifted amateurs who held a guide's diploma, but did not practise professionally. Coming as he did from Geneva, Mont Blanc was his home range, and gave him a different outlook to the conservative Swiss of the Bernese and Valaisan mountain centres. He was in the forefront of modern development, because whilst he could tackle the great traditional style routes like the Diable Ridge he was not averse to the new vogue for *nordwands*.

The notoriety which the Austro-German climbers of the 'thirties attracted with their extreme climbs tends sometimes to overshadow the fact that other nationalities were involved. In September, 1931, Roch, with his companion Robert Gréloz, made the first ascent of the steep ice wall forming the North Face of the Aiguille de Triolet, and in the following year the same two climbers made a daring unorthodox descent of the North Face of the Dru, using several hundred feet of rope. The descent took two days and they suffered a storm during the night. One rope was cut by a falling stone and another jammed and had to be abandoned. Roch's descent of the Dru roused the editorial wrath of the conservative *Alpine Journal*: 'This degradation of the peak is undoubtedly the most revolting and unsportsmanlike travesty of mountaineering yet reported in this journal.'

The early years of climbing are reflected in this picture of the Aig. Verte; **A:** Petit Dru; **B:** Grand Dru; **C:** Aig. Verte; **D:** Les Droites; **E:** Aig. du Moine; **F:** Charpoua Glacier; **G:** Telèfre Glacier; **1:** Whymper's route 1865; **2:** Miss Stratton and Miss Lloyd's route 1871; **3:** Middlemore's party 1876; **4:** Dent's route, 1878; **5:** the guides' route 1879; **6:** Mummery's route 1881.

Above: A bivouac on the Chamonix Aiguilles. The prominent square tower with turrets is the Grépon.

Left: The Grand'mère Crack on the Ryan-Lochmatter route on the East Ridge of the Plan, first climbed in 1906 by V.J.E. Ryan with the guides Franz and Josef Lochmatter.

But there was a new spirit abroad, not only in the Mont Blanc range, but throughout the Alps. A star had risen in the East and men followed it, though not all the men were wise.

Willo Welzenbach was born in Munich in 1900, the son of a senior railway official. In 1921 he joined the elite Munich Academic Alpine Club where he soon became a star performer, repeating all the hardest rock climbs in the Northern Limestone Alps. During this period he became convinced that the fourfold grades of difficulty which Hans Dülfer had introduced in the early years of the century were no longer sufficient for modern rock climbing and in 1926 he proposed a scale of I–VI (following the grades given in German school examinations!) which, with some modifications, became the basis for grading throughout the Alps.

Welzenbach's interest extended to all aspects of the mountain scene, and indeed, his doctoral thesis dealt with snow structures and avalanches.

Meanwhile, he had also been giving some thought to ice-climbing, currently in the doldrums. It is true that some very steep, even dangerous, climbs had been done, such as the Cordier Couloir on the Verte, but on the whole ice-climbing lagged behind rock-climbing in technical difficulty. Welzenbach came up with a startling concept: *Why not treat ice climbs as if they were rock climbs?* In other words, attack the ice positively, working out a route as one would on rock. In this way of thinking even the steepest ice faces were theoretically possible and what is more, steep ice and steep rock could be combined to give some very hard 'mixed' routes. This opened up a whole new world to the climber: all the great faces of the Alps.

Protection was an obvious problem. On rock one could use pitons, but on ice? It was Welzenbach's friend Fritz Rigele who came up with the answer – a long barbed spike which could be driven into the ice. So the ice piton became an indispensable aid in modern alpinism.

In 1924, the year of his graduation, Welzenbach and Rigele put theory into practice and climbed the extremely steep North-West Face of the Gross Wiesbachhorn in the Austrian Alps. During the next two years Welzenbach followed this up with a remarkable series of *nordwands* in the Eastern Alps and around Zermatt. British traditionalists were infuriated: 'senseless variations – if a face can be climbed at all it can be climbed anywhere' was their general response. It didn't help matters when the French climber Lucien Devies pointed out that the capital of the mountaineering world had been transferred from London to Munich.

When Welzenbach came to the Mont Blanc area in 1926, however, it was to rock he turned. He had set his sights on the unclimbed South Ridge of the Aiguille Noire de Peuterey – an obvious 'last great problem' if ever there was one.

I described in Chapter 4 how the two great ridges of this impressive mountain enclose a hollow known as the Fauteuil – the armchair. Looking up from the Fauteuil the ridge on the right is the original way of climbing the peak, discovered by Wentworth back in 1877: the ridge on the left is the South Ridge; a series of towers marching up to the summit, like teeth on the edge of a saw. Even from below it looks extremely difficult and, for once, appearances don't lie.

The first tower on the ridge is known as the Pointe Gamba (3067m). It was first climbed by Paul Preuss and Ugo di Vallepiana in 1913, but the gap between it and the next part of the ridge is such that it can be regarded as a quite separate climb. The South Ridge climb proper starts beyond the gap and was first attempted by Guido Mayer and Angelo Dibona, also in 1913. They managed to reach the crest of the ridge low down, at about 3000 metres, when they were driven back by bad weather.

This was the state of play when Welzenbach, with his companion Eugen Allwein, made their attempt thirteen years later. At 2.30 am on July 23 they left the small hut which had been constructed in the Fauteuil three years earlier and made their way by moonlight across to the ridge. They expected to complete the climb in the day, possibly returning down the ordinary ridge route by moonlight next night, but unfortunately, built into their plans was a cardinal error – they started *below* the Pointe Gamba, which they intended to climb or bypass as the occasion demanded. In fact, they managed to bypass it by a circuitous route, which took four precious hours.

They now embarked on an amazing ridge, where steep rock steps alternated with short easy stretches. Time and again they were forced to traverse to avoid obstacles, but always working up the ridge. At one stage Welzenbach tried to overcome an overhang by throwing a rope over a block above, but in attempting this he wrenched his shoulder out of its socket. This painful occurrence seems to have been a frequent disability of Welzenbach's, so he had no compunction about jerking the arm back into its socket and continuing the climb – though he did allow Allwein to retain the lead from then on.

Eventually they came to a smooth tower which forced them to traverse right before some difficult slabs allowed them to reach its top. The time was three pm, the height 3355 metres. They could not go on. The ridge ahead bristled with difficulties. From where they stood the next pitch seemed to be an abseil from the tower into a gap, and once they had abseiled retreat would be problematical, even impossible. This was a risk for which they were not prepared. Slowly they picked their way back, abseiling where they could in order to save time. Even so, darkness overtook them on the ridge and it was three am before they reached the hut, almost twenty-five hours after they had left it.

Some years later Pointe 3355m was christened Pointe Welzenbach in Willo's honour.

Welzenbach never returned to the Noire. Instead, the struggle was taken up by a group of local aspirant guides who felt that the South Ridge belonged to Courmayeur and were determined to make it their own. Between 1926 and 1930 several attempts were made which succeeded in reaching the next tower, now called Pointe Brendel (3497m), though not in climbing it. The Italians were poorly equipped with old fashioned, heavily nailed boots and they suffered bad weather.

It was two of Welzenbach's compatriots who eventually succeeded. Karl Brendel and Hermann Schaller climbed the ridge on August 26–27, 1930. It was the first great triumph in the Western Alps for the new Munich School, the beginning of what has been called 'the final conquest of the Alps'. Many of the leading Continental climbers were eager to repeat the climb – Giusto Gervasutti, Gabriele Boccalatte, Lucien Devies, Laurent Grivel, Nina Pietrasanta were amongst those who succeeded. Both Brendel and Schaller were killed in the year following their famous victory, Brendel in the Eastern Alps and Schaller on the German expedition to Kangchenjunga, and the South Ridge itself became something of a grim symbol for the new wave of climbers for, as André Roch pointed out, out of thirty climbers who succeeded in climbing it more than half were later killed on other mountains.

In the autumn of 1926, Welzenbach began to suffer severe pains in his right arm, probably from some tuberculosis of the bone. He underwent surgery and spent five months recuperating in Switzerland, but the arm was left permanently weakened. He was soon back in the mountains, however, and though his weak arm was supposed to preclude severe rock-climbing, he felt confident enough in 1927 to try the Hirondelles Ridge of the Grandes Jorasses, though without success. It was climbed a few days later by an Italian party led by the guide Adolphe Rey, who overcame the crux pitch, now called the Fissure Rey, using three pitons.

That same summer Welzenbach also reconnoitred the Brenva Face of Mont Blanc, the first ascent of which was also to take place later in the season. The reconnaissance consisted of climbing the Old Brenva. The original route of 1865 was still regarded as a difficult climb by most mountaineers, but Welzenbach realised that modern techniques and modern attitudes were outstripping the climbs of yesteryear and relegating them to their proper place in history. The Old Brenva, he said, had become 'a comfortable half-day outing'. Few climbers would go so far, even today, but one takes the point.

In 1930, Welzenbach, with his companions Fritz Rigele and Karl Wien, had a look at the North Face of the Grandes Jorasses. Due to persistent bad weather the buttresses were out of condition but they saw the possibilities of the huge icy flanks to the left of the main buttresses, now called the Shroud. They crossed the bergschrund but were forced to retreat when they found themselves on unclimbable ice-covered slabs. Three years later Welzenbach returned to the Shroud, but with no more success. Like all his contemporaries, however, he was impressed by the challenge of the Grandes Jorasses' North Face, though he was destined to play no part in its ultimate conquest.

Apart from his outstanding climbs in the Eastern Alps, Welzenbach's reputation as the father of modern ice-climbing was to rest principally on the series of great north faces he climbed in the Oberland in 1932 and 1933, but in the year preceding these he undertook his most dangerous and controversial climb: the North Face of the Grands Charmoz.

The North Face of the Charmoz is the one which can be seen so easily from Montenvers, frowning down on the Mer de Glace which lies in the trench below. On the far side it is limited by the huge North-East Ridge, distinguished by the spearlike subsidiary summit known as the Aiguille de la République, whilst on the near side, the limit is the main crest line of the North-West Ridge descending from the mountain's summit towards another pinnacle, the Doigt de l'Etala, and a col of the same name. Three distinct parts go to make up the face: steep slabs, which occupy the lower half, then an icefield, not quite so steep, which funnels up to a broad central couloir cutting through the summit headwall, which makes the third part. Below the face lies the small Thendia Glacier.

Ryan and the Lochmatters had wandered onto the upper portion of the face back in 1905 when they were trying to climb the ridge from the Col de l'Etala and in 1926 two French climbers, Paul Fallet and R. Tezenas du Montcel, had had a desperate retreat from high up on the face when they were struck by a storm – an episode described by the *Alpine Journal* as 'an ennobling story of comradeship in peril'.

In 1931 Welzenbach attempted the face accompanied by his friend Willy Merkl, another distinguished Munich climber. At dawn on June 30 they crossed a fragile snow bridge which took them from the Thendia Glacier onto the face and at once found themselves engaged in delicate rock-climbing comparable, Welzenbach thought, with some modern routes in the Eastern Alps. Merkl led, in deference to his partner's weak arm.

As they slowly gained height, avalanches rumbled down gullies to right and left, water trickled down the cracks they climbed, and stones whirred ominously over their heads from the icefield above.

By mid-afternoon they had reached the icefield but this was now so slushy from the heat of the day that they dared not continue up it, so they decided to bivouac, giving the ice a chance to freeze again overnight. Next morning, after a scanty cup of tea, they cramponned up the ice to reach its top edge by eight am.

The logical continuation of the climb was to follow the central gully through the headwall to the summit ridge, but Welzenbach

133

and Merkl thought the danger from falling stones was too great. Instead, they opted to find Ryan's route on the slabby rocks right of the gully. Unfortunately, they veered too far to the right and ended up on the North-West Ridge, at a cairn which probably marked the highest point of exploration, for the ridge had not been climbed at that time.

The two Germans were in a dilemma. Either they could return onto the face to try and find the proper way or they could complete the North-West Ridge, which looked fearsomely difficult (it wasn't climbed until 1950), in which case they would have hybridised two routes into an unsatisfactory whole. As it happened, gathering storm clouds took the decision out of their hands and they descended to suffer a miserable storm-lashed bivouac on the Doigt de l'Etala.

Back at Montenvers, Welzenbach and Merkl's competitive edge was honed by finding their friends Anderl Heckmair and Gustl Kröner also had plans to attack the Charmoz. Welzenbach and Merkl were determined to be first.

And so, on July 5, they set out again for the North Face to pick up the route where they had left off, so to speak. They climbed up to the Col de l'Etala in glorious weather and bivouacked on the North-West Ridge, then, at six the next morning launched themselves onto the icefield. They traversed across the central gully, where they were bombarded by stonefall, and tried to climb a ramp to the left of it, but found that this too was in the line of fire. Forced further left still along outward sloping rock bands, glazed with ice, they found themselves on the ridge of a tall pillar.

So engrossed had they been with the climbing and the stonefall that they had scarcely noticed the deteriorating weather. Now they climbed faster, hoping to reach the summit before the weather broke, but it was a forlorn hope. Just as they reached a tiny stance, the rain and hail struck them with full fury, pinning them to the rock for three hours, unable to move. Not until late afternoon did the storm relent sufficiently to allow them to continue their ascent. That night they bivouacked on a small ledge below the crest of the North-East Ridge, about halfway between the Aiguille de la République and the summit of the Charmoz. They were to spend the next sixty hours trapped on their cramped eyrie.

Storm followed storm relentlessly, like some mad *son et lumière* played out for hours on end in drenching rain, freezing hail, or soft, deadly snowfalls. Powder snow began to pour down the wall behind their bivouac tent, almost forcing them off the ledge. A conscious effort had to be made to crawl from beneath their cover and clear the snow away.

Though they had little to eat they felt no hunger; only an overwhelming thirst which no amount of snow seemed to satisfy. They spoke little, each man concerned with his own thoughts, occasionally scribbling a note in his diary. They wondered how the news that they were 'missing' was being received by their friends and fervently hoped that no rescue was being attempted.

Towards evening on the fourth day the sky lightened a little, bringing false hope, for the blizzard returned with all its old fury. Their spirits sank, their bodies ached with cramp and the intense cold gnawed into the marrow as they spent a miserable fourth night on the face.

Relief came next day with a morning of clear skies and warm sun, but it was relief tempered with anxiety, for already clouds were beginning to gather round the summit of the Aiguille Verte across the Mer de Glace, which the two men recognised as a sign of more bad weather. They realised they would have to move quickly, to take advantage of the fine spell, and yet they were frustrated on all sides. The rocks were covered in fresh snow and glazed with ice, which made progress both difficult and dangerous, and they themselves creaked like old men until their limbs loosened up a bit.

Inch by inch they crept up the steep wall to the crest of the North-East Ridge. It took them four hours and they were just in time, because the moment they reached the ridge another snow storm swept over the mountain. They battled their way up the ridge to the final tower, the storm swirling round them. They knew that come what may they had to fight on; another bivouac would have been fatal. Summoning all their reserves of energy they crawled up the last tower to reach the summit of the Grands Charmoz at three pm. The last hundred metres had taken them nine hours.

They scarcely paused at the summit. Safety had not yet been won; they had to get off the mountain – and get off before dark.

Scrambling along the ridge of the Charmoz by icy chimneys and snow-filled gullies they came at last to their line of descent, the deep rift of the Charmoz-Grépon Couloir which would take them down to the Nantillons Glacier. But the couloir is broad and the thick mist made it confusing. Time and again the two tired men found themselves in a blind alley, forced to climb back up and try another line. Fresh snow piled up on the ledges and made the couloir a nightmare but as daylight began to fade they jumped the wide bergschrund onto the Nantillons Glacier.

By compass they trudged a weary path down the glacier, frustrated by crevasses which forced them into detours until at last they reached a rocky outcrop known as the Rognon, where in those days there was a small shelter. Here they rested awhile, then, gathering together the last ounce of their strength, staggered off the glacier and back along the short path to Montenvers. They entered the hotel exactly 110 hours after leaving it. And just in time to prevent any rescue attempts.

The world's press gave the ascent of the Charmoz North Face the full treatment. It was an epic of survival which not only had a happy outcome, but a triumphant one, too, since Welzenbach and Merkl had overcome everything to reach the summit. Such unaccustomed publicity for climbing alerted some climbers to the value of such publicity; it also alerted newsmen and their editors to the new wave of extreme climbing, guaranteed to bring drama and death to titillate their readers.

There were, however, more sober assessments to be made of the climb itself. First of all, Welzenbach and Merkl made an error of judgement over the final wall. When their friends Heckmair and Kröner repeated the climb about three weeks later they did the whole face in just seven hours, utilising the central couloir which their compatriots had avoided. Secondly, doubts were expressed about the validity of the ascent since it was not continuous, but done in two stages, with a descent in between. It was a tactic repeated several times in later years with harder climbs, but one which has never been wholly accepted by the climbing fraternity. Still, Welzenbach and Merkl are credited with the first ascent and the climb was, of course, a supreme epic of endurance, willpower and skill pushed to the limit. The pity of it was that the message it gave to too many eager young men was that willpower conquers everything. They forgot about the skill and endurance.

Willo Welzenbach and Willy Merkl died on the disastrous German expedition to Nanga Parbat in 1934, which cost nine lives. Once again they were called on to survive a storm, but this time even their endurance and willpower were not enough.

In an obituary notice, Lucien Devies wrote, 'Undoubtedly with Willo Welzenbach's death the greatest and most important mountaineer of the post-war period has passed on.'

8 'This is not alpinism – this is war!'

There have been many instances when the chance sight of a mountain photograph has stimulated the desire of a climber to conquest, but it must be unusual for anyone to be stimulated into action by a novel. Yet such was the case with Thomas Graham Brown, middle-aged Professor of Physiology at the University of Wales. Once he had read A. E. W. Mason's story, *Running Water*, with its dramatic climax on the Brenva Ridge, he became fascinated by the Brenva Face of Mont Blanc. Brown dreamed of climbing, not the ridge he had been reading about, but the great wall of rock and ice to the left of it. It was a remarkable ambition, for at that time Graham Brown had done no Alpine climbing whatsoever.

He was forty-two when he began his Alpine career in 1924, though he had done some climbing in Britain. He was small, with very short legs and even shorter temper; not a good technical climber, but extremely strong in will and body. He was slow on a mountain, but a friend described how he had the remarkable capacity of keeping the same pace throughout, even at the end of a long expedition, when the rest of the party were dog tired and seeking every opportunity for a rest.

It was 1926 when he first saw the mountain face which had so inspired him – and it was not at all what he had imagined. In his mind's eye he had built up a picture of the head of the Brenva Glacier as a wide bowl with a steep mountainside rearing up around the rim, curving in a snowy arc from Mont Maudit on the right to Mont Blanc on the left, or so he later claimed, though as a scientist and one who was fastidious over detail, it is difficult to understand why he didn't check it out beforehand. Nobody had actually been on the face up to that date, but it is clearly seen from various vantage points round about and there were plenty of photographs in existence. It is a curious anecdote – but then, Graham Brown was a curious chap altogether.

The Brenva Face is much more compressed than Brown had

pictured it. Imagine a funnel, or tun-dish, cut in half vertically and the spout removed, and you have a general idea of its shape. On its right, looking up from the Brenva Glacier, is Moore's Brenva Ridge of 1865 – the Old Brenva – on its left is the Peuterey Ridge, which here is marked by a huge cornerstone of rock and ice known as the Eckpfeiler Buttress. The snowy dome of Mont Blanc's summit crowns the centre of the face, with that of Mont Blanc de Courmayeur further to the left. Descending from these domes, and trapped between the Old Brenva and the Eckpfeiler is a seemingly vertical wilderness of rock and ice, hard to match anywhere else in the Alps.

In fact, like the sides of the tun-dish, it slopes. At first it is difficult to distinguish particular features, apart from the long central Great Couloir. On the right of the couloir is a shallow ridge at the foot of which is a red tower, the Sentinelle Rouge. On the left of the couloir there is a longer, more continuous ridge, which forms the Route Major, and well to the left of that again is a big buttress which, with a little imagination, can be recognised as the Pear Buttress. High up, strung between the various ridges and buttresses, are massive sérac walls which periodically, and especially at dawn, peel off terrifying ice avalanches to roar down the face.

So the attractions are obvious, but the Brenva guards its attractions well. It is not an easy place to reach. Right and left the Brenva Glacier has high barrier walls, the Frontier Ridge and Peuterey Ridge respectively, neither of which is easy to cross and the glacier itself is fantastically fractured with crevasses and séracs. It is possibly because of this that nobody had actively investigated the Brenva Face, though a number of climbers had noted the possibilities, including Preuss, Mallory and Welzenbach. The first to do so seems to have been the English climber R. W. Lloyd who made the first *descent* of the Old Brenva in 1912, having climbed it the previous year. Like most of the others, his attention was drawn to the long, buttressed ridge of the Route Major as the obvious line of ascent and it was on this, too, that Graham Brown's ambition became fixed. For someone who was little more than a novice it was a daring ambition – the Old Brenva itself had only been climbed twenty times in the sixty-two years since it was first done – and Brown was hardly in the Welzenbach class.

Yet he came to the Alps in 1927 prepared to tackle the Brenva Face if the opportunity arose and arise it did, for Fate brought him a redoubtable partner, Frank Smythe. They were thrown together at the end of the holiday period when their original companions returned home, otherwise it is highly unlikely that they would have joined forces, for Smythe was a very good climber indeed. Earlier that season he and J. H. B. Bell had made the second ascent of the Ryan-Lochmatter route on the Plan, he had followed George Bower up the Knubel Crack on the Grépon and he had climbed the Old Brenva.

It was Smythe's first season of mountain freedom. He had thrown up his job as an engineer, hoping to earn a living writing about mountains and photographing them. On both counts he was destined to be very successful, for he was a superb photographer and his books proved immensely popular with the general public. While in the Himalaya he was to climb Kamet in 1931, at 7745 metres the highest summit then attained, and on Everest in 1933 he equalled the highest altitude reached in the pre-war years.

This great ability, however, was offset by a touchy temperament – Ivan Waller tells the story of how he once climbed with Smythe all day and at the end of it addressed him innocently as Frank, only to receive a frosty rebuke: 'Less of the Frank – I'm Mr Smythe to you.' Raymond Greene, who climbed with him in the Himalaya and knew him well, said that Smythe was the only person he knew whose temper improved with altitude.

It was a potentially explosive combination: the middle-aged novice, the young expert (Smythe was twenty-seven), and neither of them known for the sweetness of their natures. To compound the mischief, when they set off for the Brenva each had his own idea of what it was they were going to climb. Brown, of course, had the Route Major firmly in mind but Smythe simply wanted to make a variation on the Old Brenva. In the end they did neither, but settled for a compromise route which lay between the two, on the right of the Great Couloir. They bivouacked for the night by the distinctive rock, the Sentinelle Rouge, then next day climbed a branch of the couloir and a twisting rib of rock above it to the final sérac barrier which they feared might be a major obstacle. But it went easily enough and by late afternoon they were on the summit of Mont Blanc, having made the first breach in the Brenva Face without any undue heroics, or even without any prior planning. They called the route the Sentinelle Rouge, after the rock where they had bivouacked.

It should have been a matter of mutual rejoicing but given the two men involved perhaps that would be expecting too much. Smythe made no secret of the fact that he regarded the climb as his creation and that only his superior skill had got Brown up the route at all. Brown was disappointed that they had not attempted the Route Major and he later objected to some of Smythe's published descriptions of the climb. Certainly Smythe had no intention of ever climbing with Graham Brown again.

Yet despite their mutual antipathy, the unresolved challenge of the Route Major inevitably drew them together again the following season. Brown was so keen on the route that he would have climbed with the Devil himself if he thought it necessary and Smythe, equally keen by now, felt honour bound to ask Brown to join him, since it was his idea in the first place. Smythe, however, tried to dilute the inevitable friction by making up a party of four for the climb, but the other two dropped out. In Chamonix that summer of 1928, both men secretly and desperately sought other partners for the big climb but without success.

And so the evening of August 6 saw the two once again at their bivouac under the Sentinelle rock. Conditions were very different from the previous year: then, a poor season had left plenty of snow consolidated on the face but now, after a dry season, there was much less snow and the crossing of the ice slopes to the Sentinelle had been tricky.

The chief difficulty was an avalanche channel, four metres deep with overhanging sides, which they had to cross. With Brown belaying him, Smythe lowered himself into the channel, but suddenly the thin lip broke off, Smythe jerked back onto the rope and in the excitement of the moment let go of his ice axe. He found himself hanging in the channel, his axe out of reach. Nor could his companion reach it, and a careless flick of the rope might send the axe skittering down the face, lost forever. That would certainly have been the end of the expedition.

Brown lowered Smythe into the bed of the channel where he was able to stand on the thirty-degree slope because of his crampons. But he couldn't do much else; he certainly couldn't climb the overhanging ice walls of the channel without his axe. There was nothing for it but that Brown must leave his secure belay to try and rescue Smythe's axe. One false move and both would slide off into eternity.

Brown pushed his own axe as deeply as he could into the snow, passed a turn of the rope round the shaft, and delicately edged his way to the avalanche groove. At last he reached the lost axe and, lying full stretch on the ice slope, tried to pass it down to Smythe. But the channel was too deep and Smythe could not reach it. Desperately Smythe grasped the rope and hauled himself a few inches up the channel wall until his clutching fingers managed to close on the axe. Fortunately for both of them, Brown's axe held firm.

Once more in possession of his ice axe, it wasn't long before Smythe managed to climb out of the other side of the channel and take a firm stance. Their troubles were not yet over. The only way that Brown could get into the deep channel was to drop in, trusting to the rope to hold him. He landed with a sickening jolt. For a moment he thought all was well, then his feet shot from under him and he went sliding down the channel as if on some mad Cresta Run. The rope came taut and the slide was halted. Smythe's belay was a good one.

It was a thankful pair of climbers who bivouacked that night under the Red Sentinel.

They rose at four next morning and after a breakfast of biscuits and cocoa made a cache of some spare food and fuel in case they had to retreat. An hour later they set off to cross the Great Couloir towards their promised ridge. For a few minutes they were exposed to great avalanche danger from the pendulous ice cliffs near the top of the face, but at last Brown was on the ridge he had dreamed about for so long! At first they scrambled up some easy rocks, then avoided the first big buttress by descending into the Great Couloir again and creeping up its edge until they could once more get onto the rocks. Before long they came to a narrow snow arête, similar to the one on the Old Brenva, except that this one did not run out onto snow slopes at the top end but terminated sharply against the red granite of another rock buttress. The thin arête was delicate and the buttress, though easy enough, was made more difficult by a glazing of ice on the rocks. But by 8.45 am they were sitting on top of the buttress, preparing to eat their second breakfast of sardines, bread and chocolate. Their altitude was 4120 metres, and they estimated that they were about halfway up the climb.

Two more snow arêtes now followed, longer but broader than the first and separated by a rock outcrop. Beyond, they could see the huge final buttress and wondered how they could climb it.

From the end of the final arête they climbed up to an icy shelf and surveyed the prospects for the buttress, which rose in two tiers to a height of some 120 metres. They were below the junction of two faces. On the left the more amenable face was split by a chockstone chimney which is nowadays usually used as the way up but the two pioneers rejected it, thinking it too difficult. Further left still, any route would be menaced by the séracs of the ice wall which topped the buttress and so that too was rejected. The only possible way seemed over to the right, where the buttress was overhanging but might be turned by a flanking movement.

They climbed an ice slope to a corner where a tongue of rock met the overhanging walls of the buttress. Here there was a chimney, ice choked, but only four metres high and obviously the key to any outflanking movement. Whilst Brown belayed in the corner, Smythe tried the crack but found that under the prevailing conditions it was much too icy to climb by ordinary means. Yet the thing was short and there were good holds above if only he could reach them. Brown suggested he give Smythe a shoulder.

The manoeuvre was as grotesque as it was hazardous. They were perched on tiny steps at the top of a steep ice slope, squeezed into a tight black corner where one wall overhung and the other seemed permanently ice coated. In this precarious position, Brown bent double and jammed his shoulder into the crack for added security whilst Smythe, who was wearing crampons of course, clambered onto his back and fought to reach the holds above. But unfortunately the holds were not as good as they seemed; they too were filled with ice. Smythe, committed, could do little but fall off. With a warning cry he landed on top of his companion. Fortunately, the height involved was only a matter of inches, but the sharp spikes of one of his crampons tore off Brown's left pocket, sending his pipe

143

and tobacco into space. The other crampon stabbed into Brown's side, through his leather jacket, though fortunately not deeply. For a moment both men were a tangle of clothes and crampons until Smythe managed to free himself and slide carefully off Brown's back to some steps cut in the ice.

They must have looked like some bizarre music hall act, but it could have all gone wrong, had Smythe gone hurtling down the ice or had he slashed Brown seriously with his crampons. Incredible though it may seem after this performance they actually repeated the manoeuvre, but the other way round, with Brown climbing onto Smythe's back.

All these antics met with singularly little success. The corner was just not climbable. The alternative was to descend the ice alongside the rocky tongue which formed one wall of the corner, until one could traverse round below the tip of the tongue and climb up the other side. One can't help feeling that this is what they should have done in the first place, for though Brown describes the horrors of its steepness and claims Smythe wanted to abandon the climb rather than attempt the traverse, the difficulty seems exaggerated. The slope is a steepish fifty degrees. In any event Smythe lowered Brown down the ice and round the tongue, then followed. Brown, describing this in his book, *Brenva*, was inordinately proud of how he had cut the steps in the hard, steep ice. 'Smythe at last came into view . . . he enlarged my steps and also cut one or two new ones, and what he said during the exposed and delicate movement was proof of the deep impression which this part of the climb was making on him.' Actually, Smythe was cursing Brown for taking so long over a simple step-cutting job. The climb was doing nothing to relieve their mutual dislike – so much for the spirit of the hills.

Once they had turned the rock tongue the buttress offered little resistance. They were on its crest by 5.55 pm to find the formidable ice barrier which stretches across the Brenva cliffs was at this point virtually non-existent. The way to the top was clear! Through crusted snow they tramped up to the saddle between Mont Blanc and Mont Blanc de Courmayeur which Brown had named Col Major. Originally it had been his intention to bivouac here and descend the other side of the col next day, thus making a good old-fashioned traverse of the sort that by then only the British were still contemplating. But the

imbers on the Rochefort Arête, a classic ridge traverse first done around the turn of the century. Mont Blanc and the Brenva ce dominate the picture, with the steep ice of the North Face of the Aig. Blanche to the left.

steep ice climb, the North Face of the Aig. Blanche de Peuterey, first achieved by the Italians Chabod and Grivel in 1933.

Above: Finishing out on the Right-Hand Pillar of Brouillard, a modern route on a remote face.

Left: Walter Bonatti, unquestionably the greatest mountaineer of his generation who dominated Mont Blanc climbing.

wind was keen and the desire to bivouac evaporated. They wandered up to the top of Mont Blanc de Courmayeur, then returned across Mont Blanc and descended the Bosses Ridge to the Vallot Hut by nine pm.

Frank Smythe and Graham Brown never climbed together again and were scarcely on speaking terms for the rest of their lives. Both men claimed Route Major as his own invention, and when Smythe saw the first draft of Brown's proposed book, *Brenva*, he threatened to take the author to court. The book was substantially redrafted, though it still plays down the role of Smythe. In 1933, with the Swiss guides Alexander Graven and Josef Knubel (of Grépon fame), Brown went on to climb a third route on the face by means of the great Pear Buttress which he called, appropriately, Via della Pera. These three routes represent a unique tour de force by Graham Brown, perhaps the only instance where one man has taken part in every major route on an important face. For his three routes are the only real routes, such variants as exist are of little importance.

Many of the leading Continental climbers were at once attracted to the Brenva Face, anxious to repeat these new routes. The Sentinelle, in particular, was a favourite, and by the time the Via della Pera was first climbed in 1933, the Sentinelle had had five ascents. Nobody had managed to repeat Route Major, though the great German climbers Anderl Heckmair and Gustl Kröner tried and failed, so Brown repeated it himself with the guides Alexander Graven and Alfred Aufdenblatten. It was 1937 before anyone else climbed Route Major, when the great Oberland guide Hermann Steuri led Dr A. Bauer to success. In that year too, Robert Gréloz and André Roch managed to repeat Via della Pera.

The Brenva is unusual insofar as the successful climbers were British in a period when British Alpine climbing was at a low ebb. The new spirit so admirably represented by Welzenbach found no echo in English hearts; instead it was condemned in every way; it courted danger for danger's sake; it was publicity seeking; it was influenced by Fascist politics – in short, it was a thoroughly bad thing. Most of this criticism was true.

The trouble was that the real spirit had been overlaid, even corrupted, by exhibitionism and exaggerated by the press. Courting danger? Even the great Heckmair once declared in the teeth of the storm, 'Others turn back, but us – never!' And he wasn't alone in such boasts. Publicity? René Chabod, who with Gabriele Boccalatte, formed a very strong Italian team at the time, once wrote, 'One day while we were studying the face, I asked him: If we were certain that nobody would ever hear of our having conquered it, should we yet try to scale it? *Neither of us dared to reply.*' Mummery and Young would have sympathised. As for Fascism, or National Socialism, it permeated everything in those days on the Continent. Some had closer links; Welzenbach's great friend Rigele was Hermann Goering's brother-in-law; and altogether there was a good deal of *Stürm und Drang* in the Alpine air, sometimes quite literally. Great Alpine faces became battlegrounds, where men flung themselves against the mountain and the elements, and not a few died. Armand Charlet best summed it up when he described the struggle for the North Face of the Grandes Jorasses: '*Ce n'est pas de l'alpinisme, ça, c'est la guerre.*'

The splendid North Face of the Grandes Jorasses was without doubt the finest prize the Mont Blanc range had to offer to this new wave of climbers, and they knew it. It is an impressive sight – possibly the most impressive of all Alpine faces – strongly sculpted into bold, slanting buttresses of formidable power and arrogance. Two in particular catch the eye; the long straight column of the Walker Spur descending from the highest summit, Pointe Walker and the broader, slabbier buttress descending from the Pointe Croz, a little to the right as you face the mountain. Between the two is a wide gully, with Pointe Whymper above it and to the left of the Walker Spur is a steep, ice-coated wall, stretching from the glacier to the Hirondelles Ridge and known appropriately as le Linceul – the Shroud. At the Walker Spur the height of the face is 1200 metres.

The Leschaux Glacier drains the face; a broad crevassed bowl below the towering rocks which narrows into an ice stream flowing down to join the Mer de Glace. On its eastern bank stands the Leschaux Hut, the base for any attack upon the face.

Ever since 1907, when Young and Knubel first nosed around the foot of the wall, the North Face of the Grandes Jorasses, and especially the Walker Spur, was a conquest to be dreamed about. It wasn't until 1928, however, that anyone put it to the test. In that year Armand Charlet made a reconnaissance accompanied by his fellow guide Evariste Croux, two Italian climbers, L. Gasparotto and P. Zanetti, and the American, Rand Herron. With such a large party it was unlikely anything useful could be accomplished and they soon turned back. And as we saw in the last chapter, Willo Welzenbach fared no better when he looked at the face in 1930, but in 1931 a whole wave of Munich climbers hit the Western Alps, including the Grandes Jorasses.

The first to arrive were Anderl Heckmair and Gustl Kröner, who tried the great Central Couloir between the Walker and Croz Spurs but without success. (Undaunted, they went on to repeat the North Face of the Charmoz after Welzenbach and Merkl.)

Hardly had they left Chamonix than two of their keenest rivals, Hans Brehm and Leo Rittler, arrived from Zermatt where their designs on the North Face of the Matterhorn had just been pre-empted by Franz and Toni Schmid. Fearful that Heckmair and Kröner might have beaten them to the Grandes Jorasses as well, they had rushed over to Chamonix and gone straight for the Central Couloir. A week later Heckmair and Kröner returned to the mountain to discover their mangled bodies. Brehm and Rittler had been killed outright by an avalanche. In a diary, found at their bivouac site, one of them had written. 'We are standing at the base of the N. Face. It appears quite harmless . . .'

The face continued to attract the best known names in European mountaineering: Couturier, Schmid, Boccalatte, Chabod, Charlet; but the Walker Spur seemed unattainable and the Central Couloir a death trap. In 1933 Gervasutti and Zanetti reached a considerable height on the previously untried Croz Spur. At the start of the next season Armand Charlet and Robert Gréloz got a few hundred metres higher than the Italians before they too retreated. Close behind them came Raymond Lambert and Loulou Boulaz, and then the Germans, Martin Meier and Ludwig Steinauer. None was successful.

On July 30 there were no fewer than four international ropes on the mountain. The two Germans, Rudolf Peters and Rudolf Haringer, had started up on the 28th and they were followed next day by Charlet and his fellow guide, Fernand Belin; by Gervasutti and Chabod and by a team of three unknown Austrians. Charlet soon caught up with the Germans and passed them but then decided to retreat, perhaps in view of the threatening weather. Shortly after this, Gervasutti and Chabod also caught up with the leaders, Chabod arguing volubly that if they hurried they would reach the top before the threatened storm arrived. But Gervasutti thought otherwise and so they too retreated. The Austrians, on seeing the crack French and Italian teams withdraw, decided to do likewise. Peters and Haringer decided to press on and they were last seen by watchers at the Leschaux Hut at about five pm.

The next morning a violent storm swept over the Grandes Jorasses, to be followed by another and yet another. Nobody knew what had happened to the Germans; rescue was out of the question, but it seemed unlikely that anyone could have survived such a blizzard. Peters and Haringer were given up for dead.

Three days later young Peters staggered into the Leschaux Hut. He had survived five days and four nights on the terrible face, three of them under the severest weather the mountain had known for years. His story was simple, but starkly tragic. After climbing a difficult rock barrier, the two Germans had been caught by bad weather and forced to retreat. For hour after hour they abseiled down the holdless rocks until darkness fell. Haringer unroped in order to scout out a good bivouac site. Suddenly Peters heard a cry, 'Ice!' and looked round to see his luckless companion sliding down the face. Haringer fell 550 metres to his death. Peters, alone, fought for three days and nights to descend the face; an epic of endurance. It was his first visit to the Western Alps.

Later that season another formidable climber entered the lists against the Grandes Jorasses – Edouard Frendo, at that time an instructor in the military mountaineering school at Chamonix. With his friend Maurice Fourastier, an Algerian schoolmaster, he reconnoitred the face but bad weather and various unfortunate incidents made them abandon the attempt.

That winter Rudolf Peters teamed up with Martin Meier to make a difficult climb in the Berchtesgaden Range of the Eastern Alps, intended to forge a partnership fit to tackle the Grandes Jorasses. The following June, Meier spent some time watching the great mountain face come slowly into condition, like a jealous gardener waiting for some particularly rare fruit to ripen. June was very early in the season for tackling a north face but on June 24 Meier hurried to the Chamonix Post Office and sent Peters a telegram: *Sofort – Martin.* Peters came at once.

Peters and Meier moved swiftly, expertly, talking to no one en route. But after the drama of the previous year, Peters was too well known to escape detection and word soon flew round Chamonix that the Germans were back to attempt the Jorasses again. All the other would-be combatants were caught out by the Germans' early move. Frendo immediately sent a cable to Fourastier, but it then took several days to get to Chamonix from Algeria, so in desperation he teamed up with another instructor from the mountain school. They set off at once for the Leschaux Hut to discover that the two Swiss, André Roch and Robert Gréloz, were already there, having dashed over from Geneva on hearing the news. The four men decided to combine their talents in trying to beat the Germans to a first ascent.

Unfortunately their bold plan failed almost immediately. They hadn't gone far when Gréloz had the misfortune to dislocate a shoulder and though Frendo yanked it back into position without ceremony, it was too painful for Gréloz to continue. All four men decided to retreat.

In fact there was never any chance of them catching the Germans. Even before the others left the Leschaux Hut, Peters and Meier had reached the summit of the Grandes Jorasses.

They had started their climb on June 28, up a steep slope of bare ice followed by a couloir down which water was spraying, wetting them to the skin. But they reached a comfortable bivouac spot, more or less sheltered from stonefall, though during the night one stone hit their cooking pot with a loud clang, and in the morning they found both pot and stove to be irretrievably damaged. Without so much as a hot drink they started their climb again next morning, soon reaching a second great ice slope. It was here that Peters, who was leading, demonstrated the techniques which Welzenbach had advocated: he climbed straight up the ice using the two front prongs of a special pair of crampons – prongs which stuck out at an angle and could be stab-kicked into the ice, allowing the climber to balance up on his toes. At every rope length Peters cut a step on which to rest, and belayed on one of Rigele's long ice pitons. Meier then followed rapidly, hauling himself up by the rope – not an elegant way of climbing, but speed was essential if they were to escape the worst of the stonefall.

Indeed, right in the middle of the steep ice slope they were caught by a tremendous bombardment of rocks. One carried off Peters' hat, but left him unhurt, but another swept Meier off his feet, momentarily knocking him senseless, and he was held desperately by Peters on the rope. Despite injuries to his face, Meier insisted on continuing the climb at once.

Beyond the ice slope they climbed the steep rocks which had been such a problem in 1934 and at two pm they passed the point at which Peters and the hapless Haringer had retreated. Another ice slope followed and then some of the most difficult rock on the whole route, but nothing could stop them now. They knew that the Croz Spur was theirs and that the North Face of the Grandes Jorasses was conquered. At eight pm they stood on the summit ridge, storm clouds boiling round them. Incredibly, they did not know the way off! It was not until next day, after a bivouac on the ridge, that the two Germans made their way slowly down to Courmayeur.

As the Germans left for home, other competitors turned up at the Leschaux Hut for the race which was already over. Within a few days the Croz Spur was climbed by three other parties: Gervasutti and Chabod, Raymond Lambert and Loulou Boulaz, Ludwig Steinauer and Toni Messner.

And yet, as these climbers toasted their success, they knew that the real problem of the great North Face of the Grandes Jorasses remained unsolved. It stood there, arrogant, thrusting, mocking. Eyes turned towards the Walker Spur.

In 1937 Edouard Frendo teamed up with another strong French climber, Pierre Allain, to reconnoitre the Walker Spur. They seem to have decided that Charlet's route of 1928 was the best bet, for when Allain made his attempt in the following year this is the way he followed. Frendo was not able to accompany him, but he had another good climber instead, Jean Leininger. They overcame the initial pitches but when they reached the foot of the great corner which is such a feature of the lower part of the climb, they were struck by falling fragments of ice. Bruised and battered, the two Frenchmen decided to retreat.

There now came into the picture almost by accident a young Italian climber called Ricardo Cassin, a native of Lecco on Lake

Como, where he had learned to climb on the serrated limestone pinnacles of the Grigna. In a few short years Cassin and his group, the New Italy Climbing Club, had pushed themselves to the forefront of Italian rock-climbing, particularly in the Dolomites, though there they were overshadowed initially by Emilio Comici who, with the Dimai brothers, had climbed the stupendous North Face of Cima Grande in 1933. It was Comici who taught the young Lecco climbers all about artificial climbing – that is, how to use pitons and étriers to force overhanging rock into submission – so necessary for the hard new rock climbs in the Dolomites. Cassin and his friends put the lessons to good use, first in the Grigna and Dolomites and then, in 1937, by making the first ascent of the North-East Face of Piz Badile; a dramatic granite spire in the Bregaglia Alps.

By 1938 Cassin considered that he and his friends were ready to challenge the ultimate wall of all – the notorious Eigerwand in the Bernese Oberland, where in recent years several young Germans had died in the finest exhibition yet of *Stürm und Drang*. But even as Cassin and his friends arrived in Grindelwald they heard that two Germans and two Austrians were already on the fearful wall and these men, led by Anderl Heckmair, were destined to succeed. It was only when he was on his way home after the disappointment of missing the Eigerwand that Cassin thought of the Walker Spur. He determined to attempt it as soon as possible.

But first of all he had to find it. Cassin had never been to the Mont Blanc region and he had only a hazy idea of where the Grandes Jorasses lay. However, with his friend, Ugo Tizzoni, he managed to cross the Col du Géant from Courmayeur and work his way round to the Leschaux Hut. They were very impressed by the great brooding buttresses. Cassin worked out a probable line of ascent, then they went back across the Col du Géant to pick up a third member of the party, Gino Esposito, who had been with Cassin on the Piz Badile.

The three Italians set out from the Leschaux Hut on their great adventure early on the morning of August 4, 1938. Riccardo Cassin was in the lead, then came Esposito and finally Tizzoni. The climbing quickly became difficult as they reached the great corner, then tackled ice-coated slabs. Once or twice Tizzoni slipped and fell as he tried to recover the pitons Cassin had hammered into the rock and ice; it was a difficult job, which Tizzoni did well. By evening they had reached another large corner, about 450 metres above the start of the climb and here, on a good ledge, they bivouacked for the night.

The next day the climbing was, if anything, more difficult, forcing Cassin further and further to the right away from the crest of the spur. At one point an enormous roof barred the way and though Cassin traversed below it he soon ran out of rope and was forced to call for Esposito to follow. There was no stance and belay, so Esposito sat in a pair of étriers dangling from a single peg, whilst he played the rope out to his leader. Fortunately he managed to get another piton in place to act as an anchor for the precarious rope manoeuvres which Cassin was trying out. Cassin was lowered for about twelve metres, level with a spike of rock he had spied. It was out of reach so, letting go of the rock, Cassin pushed himself across the gap, swinging on the rope like an Alpine Tarzan and grabbing for the spike. He missed. Time and again he swung across the gap until at last he was able to grab the spike and pull himself to safety.

Esposito followed his leader, but it was Tizzoni who had the most difficult job. As last on the rope, and carrying the party's baggage as well, he had to climb down and across to his companions without any assistance from the rope. It was delicate work and had he come off the consequences could have been disastrous, but Tizzoni climbed superbly and reached his friends without incident. This pitch took them five hours.

As they climbed back towards the ridge the weather began to deteriorate; snow flakes drifted down, coating the holds. Slowly they climbed to the base of a large grey tower which they had noted from below and which they knew was about two-thirds of the way up the ridge. There they bivouacked for the second night, watching a thunderstorm flash and rumble in the Chamonix valley.

As they climbed towards the summit next morning, a furious thunderstorm pinned them in their bivouac sacks for half an hour then it started to snow again and continued all the way to the top. But at three pm, August 6, Cassin and his companions stood on Pointe Walker. The Walker Spur of the Grandes Jorasses had been won by the Italians at their first attempt.

Storm prevented them from descending to Courmayeur because they didn't know the way down and could easily have gone wrong in the swirling snow and mist. So once again they bivouacked. As they came down next morning they were surprised to find quite a crowd waiting to greet them. Friends had tipped off a reporter and he had followed their climb from the Leschaux Hut with binoculars, dashing down to Montenvers each evening to telephone his story to his paper. All Europe knew that the last – and some would say the finest – of the great north walls was conquered.

9 'Small man, damn big mountain'

The First World War had had no direct effect on the Mont Blanc area because France and Italy who shared the common frontier, were allies and Switzerland, of course, was neutral. The Second World War was different: on June 10, 1940, Italy declared war on a France which was already reeling from the body blows of the German panzer divisions. The Italians pushed over the Col de la Seigne into the lonely Val des Glaciers, where there was a small French garrison, and an action was fought high up near the Col d'Enclave on June 21–22. It would be hard to imagine a more lonely, desolate, useless place for military action, particularly as the French, crumbling before the German onslaught, had already sued for peace – an armistice was declared on June 25.

Peace came again to the mountains – but it was a phoney peace, for beneath the calm surface many of the inhabitants were secretly members of the French resistance movement, the *maquis*. In August 1944 when the Allies landed on the south coast of France the *maquis* rose in support. Many units had English and American liaison officers parachuted in to help them and the result was that by August 19 virtually the whole of Haute Savoie was in the hands of the Resistance. The German garrison at Chamonix, finding itself surrounded, sent for urgent reinforcements. Twenty truck-loads of troops set out to relieve them, but these were caught at Cluses by the *maquis* and annihilated. The Chamonix garrison surrendered.

But the southern side of the range was still in German hands and the Germans were determined to fight on despite the hopelessness of their situation. On February 17, 1945, a company of Austro-German mountain troops, some seventy strong, based on the Torino Hut near the Col du Géant, attacked across the Vallée Blanche towards the Col du Midi, which was held by the French. Their aim, apparently, was to seize the col, destroy the *téléphérique* there and then use their mortars to bombard Chamonix.

154

The attack started about 1.30 am and a running dog fight developed. Shots reverberated from the high mountain walls and tracer bullets curved across the snowfields. At dawn the Germans tried to storm the col but were met by withering fire from the French dug in along the ridge. At this moment, too, a small French plane appeared and began dropping hand grenades on the demoralised Germans who retreated to the Col du Géant, leaving nine dead in the snows of the Vallée Blanche. One French soldier was killed.

The action in the Vallée Blanche has been called 'the highest fight in the world' – it took place at a height of about 3500 metres – but be that as it may, it was certainly one of the silliest. There was nothing whatever to be gained by bombarding Chamonix, even if the troops had managed to gain the Col du Midi, and the whole affair can only be construed as the act of a fanatic, gambling against the odds. We know who it was – an Austrian, Captain Singel, who met his death in the charge on the col. Three months later the war was over.

Between the wars, and after, Chamonix continued to grow. It crossed the river and filled in the meadows between the old town and the English church. Smart shops appeared, and ultimately the ubiquitous supermarkets. There was even a period between 1920 and 1930 when Chamonix was very much the in place for the society set who stayed at the Majestic, Chamonix-Palace and Casino du Mont Blanc instead of Deauville or Biarritz.

The environment was changing in other ways. In 1926 the mules finally disappeared from the Montenvers track, made redundant by the rack-and-pinion railway. About this time, too, a cable car was planned for the Col du Plan, but nothing came of it; instead, in 1927 an intermediate station was opened at Gare des Glaciers on the Pierre à l'Echelle, overlooking the Bossons Glacier. In 1938 a pilot line was carried up to the ridge of the Midi overlooking the Col du Midi, where a scientific observatory was built which is officially known as the Laboratoire de Glaciologie Alpine, but which everyone calls the Cosmiques Hut. Further development was halted by the war, but afterwards a new cable car was developed to the very summit of the Aiguille du Midi, opened in 1955. The valley now seems to sprout wires in all directions.

Today it is possible to cross from one side of the range to the other by cable car, swinging high over the Vallée Blanche. Impressive though this is as a technological achievement, it hardly helps the conservation of the mountains and cannot, in any case, be regarded as a serious form of transport. But the tunnel is. As long ago as 1787 de Saussure had said, 'A day will come when we will build a safe road through Mont Blanc and unite the valleys of Aosta and Chamonix.' This was remarkably prophetic. In 1958 work was begun on the Mont Blanc road tunnel, which has its French portal at les Pélerins at 1274 metres and its Italian counterpart at 1380 metres at Entrèves. Four years later, in September 1962, the tunnel opened to traffic, cutting many miles off the journey between Northern Europe and the Italian manufacturing cities such as Turin and Milan – and changing for ever the once peaceful village of Courmayeur. Twenty-three men died in its construction.

I suppose one could look on the tunnel as the ultimate rape of Mont Blanc, but the old mountain has been subjected to other indignities over the years. On February 11, 1914, H. Parmelin of Geneva was the first man to fly over the summit of Mont Blanc. Seven years later, on July 30, 1921, François Durafour landed his biplane 'Caudron' on the Col du Dôme and became the first pilot to land and take off from a snowfield over 4000 metres above sea level. In 1930 a pilot called Thoret flew over the Chamonix Aiguilles and managed to drop supplies to the Vallot Observatory, while at 6.30 am on June 23, 1960, Henri Giraud of Grenoble landed his Piper Cub Chouca on the very summit of Mont Blanc: a feat as daring as it is daft.

The years following on the Second World War were ones of social liberation. Better wages, better holidays, helped people to broaden their horizons. Many took up alpinism and their attitude was much more akin to that of the Munich climbers of pre-war days than to the Alpine Club ethos of long ago. Standards rose dramatically, slowly at first as Europe recovered from the war, then with a gathering momentum which has hardly stopped since. New gear, and perhaps equally, new attitudes, have made the old hard routes like the Walker Spur everyday events for competent climbers. Such is the general standard nowadays that very few new climbs are reported in the press and they are unlikely to get more than a passing mention even in the specialist magazines. Technological ingenuity is gradually overcoming every obstacle. Men and women still get killed but the odds are stacking up in favour of the climber. In the immediate post-war years the odds were still heavily in favour of the mountain.

One day in August 1949 a young Italian climber was making his way towards the Col du Géant from Chamonix when his eye fell on the cluster of pinnacles below Mont Blanc du Tacul. Chief amongst these were the fearsome-looking teeth of the Aiguilles du Diable where Charlet had so distinguished himself in the pre-war years, but below the ridge there were other, quite distinct needles of rock, one of which had a curious summit block resembling a monk's cowl, for which reason it was known as the Grand Capucin. The sheer East Face of the pinnacle seemed to the nineteen-year-old Walter Bonatti to represent the ultimate in rock-climbing, and he determined that he would be the one to climb it.

An opportunity came in the following July. With his friend Camillo Barzagli, Bonatti tackled the steep granite face of the tower but on the second day of the climb they were frustrated by storms and forced to give up. A month later he was back again with Luciano Ghigo. They spent the first night in a cave, a natural hollow in the face which served as a comfortable bivouac. There was a storm during the night and it looked as though the climb might have to be abandoned again, but next day the sky was clear, the air was warm and Bonatti and Ghigo were able to push their way up the steep face. The climbing was extremely difficult, much of it was 'artificial', involving the use of pitons or étriers. Such climbing is desperately fatiguing and as darkness fell the two Italians were glad to discover a suitable bivouac site.

The weather continued fine on the next morning and now another problem began to assail them, thirst. The hot sun beat off the granite face as though from a burnished mirror. The climbers sweated and dehydrated. Their tongues grew thick and black and they could scarcely speak. So desperate were they that when the first flurries of snow suddenly drifted down they grabbed at them to try to assuage their thirst.

Evening was drawing on. A huge slab soared up, barring their way, but above the slab was a broad snow ledge which Bonatti reckoned would make a good bivouac site for the third night. Because the slab looked difficult and because speed was essential, he divested himself of all unnecessary gear before setting off. His rucksack, his warm duvet jacket, even his waterproofs were left behind – they could be hauled up after the pitch was climbed. But the climbing was even more difficult than Bonatti had imagined. His progress slowed to a crawl. Each move had to be fought for – and night was starting to shade the rocks.

At last it was too dark to go any further. In a tiny niche which he had fortuitously discovered at the very last moment, Bonatti was forced to bivouac for the night, his warm clothes only a few unreachable feet below, as the cold bit into his bones.

Fortunately the weather remained fine during the night and dawn, too, brought promise of another hot day. It was a false promise. Before long it began to snow and soon the red granite tower was enveloped in a swirling white maelstrom. Friends, anxious about the two climbers, gathered at the foot of the pinnacle and shouted up into the storm. They heard faint replies and soon, to their relief, Bonatti and Ghigo came swinging down abseil ropes to join them. After four days of intense effort the Italians had given up; beaten by a combination of severe weather and severe difficulties.

The following July the two men returned to the Capucin. Now familiar with its intricacies, they reached their previous high point after only two days of climbing. Only the Monk's Cowl remained to be overcome.

The climbing was no easier and it was slow work inching up the steep rock. Towards evening disaster almost struck. As Bonatti moved up on a difficult step the piton on which he was standing gave a sudden, sickening jerk and flicked out of its crack. Bonatti fell but with lightning reflexes he grasped a knob of rock and held on grimly with his fingertips. Ghigo was given a brief breathing space in which to whip in the slack rope and adopt a secure stance before Bonatti's fingers uncurled and he fell a second time to be held superbly by his second.

Bonatti was uninjured but his nerves were badly shaken. He climbed down to his companion and they decided to bivouac for the night, hanging from their étriers over the void.

It snowed during the night, but a grey dawn brought relief. More difficult climbing followed until at last a final steep corner led them onto the summit of the Grand Capucin. Even now their troubles were not over. The storm came sweeping back as they descended the easier side of their peak and that evening it was two weary and almost snowblind climbers who staggered into the Torino Hut.

The climbing of the Grand Capucin was a supreme tour de force by Bonatti and Ghigo. The exposure was sensational and could only be compared with the steeper Dolomite climbs like the Cima Grande and, like the Cima Grande, the Capucin was overcome by means of continuous artificial techniques. Pitons and étriers were not unknown in the Western Alps, of course, but this was the first time they had been used on such a scale: 160 pitons were driven into the rock. It made people sit up. Here was thinking every bit as radical as Welzenbach's had been before the war but applied to rock instead of ice; Welzenbach had said treat ice-climbing like rock-climbing, and now here was a new climbing superstar, Walter Bonatti, saying treat the big walls of the Western Alps as if they were Dolomite climbs.

Bonatti's daring had opened the way to all the great rock faces of the Mont Blanc group of which none is more spectacular than the West Face of the Petit Dru. This is the smooth-looking obelisk of red granite which is so well seen from the café terrace at Montenvers. Years earlier, in 1935, the great French climbers, Pierre Allain and Robert Leininger, had made the first ascent of the North Face during which they had plenty of opportunity to study the stupendous slabs of the West Face. Allain wrote: 'The sheerness is appalling, only broken now and then by enormous overhangs. Immense faces rise smoothly for 200–300 feet without a single crack – the perfect example of the impossible.'

Even before Bonatti's success on the Capucin, French parties were trying to climb the sheer West Face of the Dru, though without much result. Rival groups from Lyons and Paris contested the face but the difficulties were such that in the end they combined forces. They did not succeed for three years, then in 1952 Guido Magnone (who despite his name is French) led a team of four climbers to the top in the most controversial of circumstances.

To overcome the West Face of the Dru, Magnone declared, it was necessary to combine the virtues of the traditional mountaineer with those of the Dolomite climber – in other words, do what Bonatti had done and use artificial techniques. Despite the example set by the Italian, this way of climbing a major peak was still regarded by the old school as the next best thing to cheating, but times were changing and what really upset the establishment was the way in which Magnone broke the climb into two separate episodes. Between July 1 and July 5 the French party climbed the lower two-thirds of the face but then they came across a difficult pendulum move which was absolutely irreversible with the equipment they had available. It was a neck or nothing situation: if they made the move then found they were unable to go on, they would not be able to get back – and they must have had in their minds the awful pre-war example of Hinterstoisser and his companions on the Eiger, who had also made an irreversible move and finding themselves trapped, had perished. The four Frenchmen retreated.

On July 16, however, they returned to the fray. Instead of repeating the lower part of the face they climbed the easier North Face until they were level with their high point of the previous attempt, then, using expansion bolts drilled into the rock, they traversed across until they could rejoin their route, which they soon completed.

Magnone's ascent of the West Face of the Dru was a great technical achievement – but was it fair? He was not the first to break a climb in two parts, of course, for the great Welzenbach had set a precedent on the North Face of the Charmoz. Nor was he the last: such methods reached their apotheosis a decade later on the Eiger Direct, where climbers were going up and down the face like yo-yos in what turned out to be a deadly circus. Nevertheless, was it fair? To which there can be no unequivocal answer. All one can say is yes, it was fair at the time in that it advanced the art of climbing, but no, it was not fair in the long run because the climb has since been done without such dubious practices. In fact, on the third ascent of the face in 1954 Joe Brown and Don Whillans did the whole thing in just over a day.

There was another consideration. Some climbers thought that

Below Mont Blanc du Tacul lies the pinnacle of the Grand Capucin, scene of one of Bonatti's early triumphs. For scale note the figures on the glacier right centre.

inset: The verticality of the East Face of the Grand Capucin is shown here. Climbers are sack-hauling on the 40-m wall, the hardest part of the climb.

The commanding Petit Dru overlooking Montenvers: **A:** Aig. Verte; **B:** Aig. Sans Nom; **C:** Petit Dru; **D:** Flammes de Pierre; **E:** Niche des Drus; **F:** couloir leading to West Face climbs; **1:** North Face climbed by Allain and Leininger 1935; **2:** West Face climbed by Beradini, Dagory, Laine and Magnone in 1952; **3:** Bonatti Pillar soloed by Bonatti 1955. Below the summit of the Verte is the line of Charlet's route on the Nant Blanc Face, one of his favourite climbs.

the route Magnone had made was not the best the face had to offer. In the first place, it missed out much of the lower part of the mountain by sidling in along some ledges, and in the second place it wandered over towards the North Face and near the top the two routes shared a common line.

One of those who thought this way was Walter Bonatti. He thought that the real challenge of the face was the splendid ridge which bounds the right edge and is known as the South-West Pillar. Impressively steep, the pillar is obviously difficult and made more so by the fact that it is guarded by a particularly nasty couloir, down which rock and ice fall at frequent intervals. The Magnone route also starts from the couloir, but lower down. To attempt the South-West Ridge meant exposure to danger for that much longer.

In the year following Magnone's triumph, Bonatti and a friend, Carlo Mauri, made an attempt on the South-West Pillar. They were not successful and Bonatti did not return until 1955 when he led a strong team consisting of Mauri, Andrea Oggioni and Iosve Aiazzi in another unsuccessful attempt, during which they survived bad weather and dramatic avalanches in the couloir. Oggioni was injured by stonefall.

During this time Bonatti was going through a crisis of self-confidence which had been exacerbated by the fairly undistinguished role he had played in the Italian ascent of K2, the second highest mountain in the world, in 1954. He had become a professional guide and yet the mountains seemed to be losing their appeal – indeed, life itself seemed to have no meaning. After the failure of his second attempt on the Dru, he reached the depths of his depression. The fact of his failure meant nothing to him and he was painfully aware that had his party succeeded on the South-West Pillar, that too would have meant nothing. He felt as though he was a spent force and people were insinuating that K2 had broken the great Bonatti.

There had to be a test. There had to be something that would prove to the world, and to himself, that climbing still had meaning for him, that the mountains were still his spiritual home, and that he was still the supreme craftsman. Suddenly, he had a wild idea: he would climb the South-West Pillar of the Dru alone and unaided.

Solo climbing was an honourable branch of the game with a

long history, but nobody had thought of soloing anything quite so ambitious as the South-West Pillar. If there had to be a test, there could hardly be a stiffer one than this.

Bonatti arrived at Montenvers on August 11 with two close friends who were to help in the initial stages. Nobody else knew of Bonatti's plan. For four days the rain swept down, obscuring the red pillar and making a start impossible, then, on the night of the 14th the sky cleared and the three men set off down the tourist ladders which lead to the Mer de Glace. Across the flat, dirty ice they trudged towards the huge bulk of the Dru which towered in front of them, black against the star-filled night sky.

A flurry of rain brushed them but it soon passed and by eight am they were in the dangerous couloir. It was now time for Bonatti to go it alone. He had prepared for this moment meticulously. He knew that to try and climb the couloir with a huge rucksack on his back made him much more of a target for missiles, so he had designed a long cylindrical sack, as tall as himself, which held the sixty pounds of gear or more he needed. This he attached to himself with a rope and the plan was that he would climb a pitch quickly because unencumbered, then pull his haul-sack up after him.

In practice it didn't work out quite as expected. Because of the dangerous nature of the couloir it was essential to climb near the side walls where there was less chance of being hit by a stone. But this in turn increased the friction on the haul-sack to such a degree that it almost weighed double. Pulling it up was exhausting work and there were times when it jammed altogether and Bonatti had to climb down to free it. After seven hours he had made only 150 metres of ascent in the couloir – and this, he knew, was the easy part. He began to despair and when the weather turned bad he decided to retreat.

Back at Montenvers Bonatti rigorously lightened his load. Out went the portable radio intended for weather reports and out too went most of the provisions. Only the essential climbing gear remained. Even so, he knew that dragging the haul-sack up the couloir would still be a strenuous business. It could take him two days and leave him exhausted even before the proper climb had begun. His agile mind looked for another way; a way which might be less dangerous and certainly less tiring.

Bonatti's ingenious solution was to climb up the Charpoua

162

Glacier, then follow the regular route up the Drus to the point where it touches the crest of the Flammes de Pierre Ridge which separates the dangerous couloir of the West Face routes from the Charpoua Glacier. From here he could abseil into the head of the couloir on the other side. Thus he would reach the top end of the couloir without having to climb it at all.

Things did not go well. The Charpoua Glacier was badly crevassed and there was a lot of fresh snow around. Bonatti and his two helpers could do no more than reach the safety of the climbers' hut on the glacier, where they spent the night of August 16. The hut book told them the grim news that conditions on the Dru were so bad that there had only been one ascent all season, even by the ordinary route. Bonatti spent the night feeling 'like a condemned man in the last hours before his execution'. To make matters worse a piton in his haul-sack punctured his fuel bottle, soaking and spoiling most of his food.

Next day, climbing alone now, he reached the crest of the ridge at 11.30 am and began the 245-metre abseil down the other side into the death couloir. The rocks were steep and ice plastered, devoid of all natural protection. Bonatti abseiled from pitons, first of all lowering the heavy sack, then spinning down the rope after it into space. At first things went well enough but then, whilst trying to hammer home an awkward piton, he missed his aim and smashed the heavy hammer into the tip of his ring finger. The blow was so hard it pulped the end of his finger and blood spurted everywhere. Bonatti felt faint and sick with the pain. Desperately he struggled to retain consciousness in order to hammer home the errant piton – it was his only protection – and to staunch the flow of blood. It was an hour before he felt able to go on and evening was closing in when at last he made his final abseil into the head of the couloir.

Now came a second blow. The abseil rope jammed and no amount of tugging would fetch it down. He could not abandon it because he needed it for the climb, but he was too weak, too tired, to climb up and release it and in any case the light was going. There was nothing Bonatti could do but chip a platform in the ice on which to stand for the night, and to pray that the deadly couloir would be frozen into stillness.

Worse was to come. He was soaking wet from the soft snow he had brushed against during his descent. He had no fuel, so that he could not make a hot drink and he spent the night shivering and hungry on his cramped ice ledge.

Fortunately the rope was easily freed next morning and at last Bonatti was able to tackle the great red pillar. His injured hand made things difficult, both for climbing and sack-hauling, and the fresh snow which plastered the rock didn't help matters either. Progress was slow, but by late afternoon he had reached the highest point he and Mauri had reached on their first attempt. He bivouacked for the second time.

Throughout the day Bonatti had been perfecting his method of sack-hauling, which, though laborious, was reasonably safe. He treated the sack as another climber, tying it to one end of a short rope and himself to the other. Leaving the sack on a ledge, he would climb up as far as was convenient, using pitons where necessary, then hammering home a good solid piton he would clip the rope into this and climb back down to the sack, removing as he did so all the previous pitons, which went back into his reserve, the top piton being protection enough. Then he climbed back again and finally hauled up the sack. In effect all this yo-yoing meant that Bonatti made the equivalent of three ascents of the route.

Next day he found himself facing a feature he called the Lizard, from its shape. The way to overcome it was by an icy chimney up which he nicked hand and footholds in some sensationally exposed climbing. At the top, however, the chimney was completely blocked by ice and overhanging. The only way Bonatti could see of overcoming this problem was to make holes in the ice then hammer a wooden wedge into each hole. In those days climbers on such serious routes as this often carried a few wooden wedges for hammering into cracks which were too wide for metal pitons. Each wedge was threaded with a nylon loop from which an étrier could be hung. Using wedges on ice was a novel expedient – the problem was that as soon as any weight was put on the wedge, the increased pressure would rapidly melt the ice. Bonatti calculated that a wedge would only hold for two or three minutes.

He hammered home the first wedge, clipped in the étrier, and gingerly pulled himself up. It was a sensational position, hanging free hundreds of metres above the glacier, but Bonatti had no time to admire the view. Furiously he hammered home the second wedge and pulled himself up a few more metres. Above him he could see an ice-free crack. Eagerly his fingers felt into the crack for purchase but at first found none. As the seconds ticked by the search became more urgent. At last, finding a mere ripple, Bonatti pulled himself up into the crack. As he did so he heard a tinkling noise behind him – the wedge he had been standing on had fallen out. It had been a close shave.

That afternoon a storm broke over the mountain, forcing him to shelter on a ledge where he decided to remain for the night. Wet and cold he was now a prey to both mental and physical exhaustion. He began talking to himself and even talking to his haul-sack as though it was a companion.

The following day he climbed a vast sheet of rock known as the Red Slabs which led to some massive overhangs which would be his next major problem. That night he bivouacked on the slabs, totally exhausted.

Bonatti faced his fifth day on the Dru in a pitiable condition. Lack of proper food and drink, bitterly cold nights and the exhausting sack-hauling were beginning to tell. His hands, one of which was bandaged of course, were lacerated and blistered from the rough rock and pulling up the sack. They were stiff and swollen and he had to exercise them before he could begin climbing. The pain was excruciating: it was all he could do not to cry out.

He was now approaching the crux of the entire route. He had to find a way round the overhangs. At first he tried to the left but found no joy there, then he tried to the right and spied a crack, thirty-six metres long, which he knew would solve the problem. If only he could reach the crack, all would be well.

The surrounding rock was incredibly smooth but Bonatti managed to place three pitons, one after the other, which helped him swing towards his goal. The last swing landed him on a narrow ledge where, to his dismay, he found there were no more piton cracks. The wall was perfectly smooth and the big crack was still twelve metres away. For several despairing moments it seemed as though he was stuck.

Then he spied a cluster of rock spikes sticking out at the foot of the crack. Could he lasso them and swing across? They were twelve metres away and a desperately small target. He tied a bunch of pitons to one end of the rope to give it weight, then swinging it like a South American *bolas*, he tried to snare the spikes. At his twelfth attempt he succeeded but it took a couple more throws to make it secure. Next Bonatti arranged a protective rope through his last piton. So now he was tied to the rope caught on the spikes and to a rope which passed in a loop through his last piton. If the spikes gave way, as seemed likely, then the rope through the piton would hold him. If the piton also gave way, which was quite possible, then he would plunge hundreds of metres to his death. It was the best he could do in the circumstances.

He launched himself across the gap, swinging on the jammed rope. Thankfully it held and Bonatti was able to swarm up and reach the crack. He pulled up his sack and drew in the second rope. Now more than ever he was committed to finishing the climb – after the pendulum there could be no going back.

The crack helped Bonatti to overcome the overhangs, but only just. It soon became icy and difficult, forcing the climber out onto the open face above the overhangs. Gradually he was circling back towards his original line and when he bivouacked that night – the fifth night he had spent on the open mountain – he was not much higher than he had been twenty-four hours earlier. The whole day had been spent circling round the jutting roofs of the overhangs. That night he saw lights flashing on the Charpoua Glacier far below and he knew it was his friends signalling. He lit a paper torch by way of reply.

By noon on the sixth day Bonatti was a mere ninety odd metres from the summit. Though the pain in his hands was excruciating and they were starting to turn septic, he knew that nothing could stop him now. He could see a party of climbers on the ordinary route and he guessed rightly that they were friends coming to meet him at the summit and congratulate him on his achievement. Everything that was not essential he dumped and for the first time in five days climbed with his sack on his back. Some overhangs delayed him and he was struck on the leg by a falling stone, but the thought of victory made him invincible.

At 4.37 pm on August 22, 1955, Walter Bonatti stepped onto the summit of the Dru. He had accomplished one of the most remarkable ascents of all time and to honour such a man climbers rechristened the South-West Pillar of the Dru the Bonatti Pillar. The climb restored Bonatti's faith in himself and the mountains. He went on to dominate Alpine climbing over the next decade.

Nor was the Dru finished as a playground. Other routes were made on it, some of which were technically more difficult than the Bonatti Pillar, though not of the same grandeur. One of these new routes was made by John Harlin, the blond American climber who was to die a decade later on the route named after him on the Eiger. Summing up how he felt about challenging the Dru, Harlin said, 'Small man, damn big mountain.'

10   Last great problem

There seemed to be no stopping Walter Bonatti. He was to Mont Blanc what Caesar was to Gaul; he came, he saw, he conquered. He began filling in the blanks on the south side of Mont Blanc where high above the Brenva, Frêney and Brouillard Glaciers huge buttresses soared, guarded by the demon of inaccessibility.

In 1957, with Toni Gobbi, he climbed the impressive Eckpfeiler Buttress, the last great bastion of the Brenva Face – the 'pillar on the edge', where the face runs into the Peuterey Ridge. It is perhaps the single most awe-inspiring piece of rock on the mountain and it is little wonder that the two Italians found the climbing difficult. They used seventy pitons and spent two nights in bivouacs before reaching the summit.

Two years later, with the closest of all his companions, Andrea Oggioni, Bonatti climbed the left-hand pillar of Brouillard, known as the Pilastro Rosso, or Red Pillar, from its distinctive colouring. The pillar is tucked away at the very head of the Brouillard Glacier, below the Pointe Louis Amédée. Even to reach it is a dangerous and difficult expedition – the Brouillard Glacier is one of the nastiest in the Alps and the face which holds the pillar is subject to stonefall. On their first attempt, Bonatti and Oggioni nearly came to grief when they were caught high up by a storm, but they were successful with their second attempt a few days later.

This seemed to be the usual pattern for Bonatti – initial failure, often under the most harrowing of circumstances, followed by ultimate success. He seemed immune to frostbite and all the other failings of the average mountaineer, able to keep functioning under the most arduous conditions, which was just as well because his luck was abominable in many cases. Yet Bonatti was not particularly well-built and, though doctors had told him he had a special resistance to cold and storm, it seems much more likely that his strength was psychological, born of rigid mental discipline. How else can one explain the extraordinary ascent of the Bonatti Pillar and later, the equally extraordinary solo ascent of the Matterhorn North Face?

The upper basin of the Frêney Glacier is trapped like a snowy amphitheatre between the great ridges of the Innominata and Peuterey. A steep icefall cuts it off from the lower glacier, though at the eastern edge of the icefall there is a way through by means of some ugly crags known as the Rochers Gruber – one of Emile Rey's discoveries back in 1880. The only other means of access is by two high cols: that on the west being the Col Eccles and that on the east, the Col de Peuterey.

Despite its high and isolated position this area of Mont Blanc's southern face was one of the first to be explored by James Eccles and his contemporaries in the 1870s. The goal in those days was the Peuterey Ridge. Nobody considered the steep granite pillars which ranged across the back of the amphitheatre and certainly not the great Central Pillar of Frêney. Eighty years on and it had become 'the last great problem' of the Mont Blanc range.

Bonatti had had his eye on the Frêney Pillar for some years, but it wasn't until 1959 that he and Oggioni made their first attempt. It wasn't successful, but his very failure alerted others to the challenge and soon the Alpine grapevine was rife with rumours of strong teams being assembled to snatch the Pillar – French, Italian, even American climbers were named. But by 1961 it still wasn't climbed and Bonatti was able to mount another attack. With him he had Oggioni, of course, and another strong Italian climber, Roberto Gallieni.

On the Sunday evening of July 7, 1961, the three Italians climbed the steep snow slopes leading up to the Fourche Hut; a small box precariously perched on the Frontier Ridge. To their great surprise they discovered the hut was already occupied by four leading French mountaineers: Pierre Mazeaud, Antoine Vieille, Robert Guillaume and Pierre Kohlmann, who were also on their way to try the pillar. Bonatti offered to withdraw since the Frenchmen were first on the scene, but they wouldn't hear of it and it was decided that the two teams would make a combined assault. Both were well equipped, though for some curious reason the French did not have any bivouac tents but relied on plastic groundsheets to keep out the cold. It was an omission which was to cost them dear.

A climbers' guidebook once described the approach to the

Central Pillar of Frêney as being a major expedition in itself. From the Fourche Hut the route leads down onto the Brenva Glacier and across it to the Col Moore, following the way to the Brenva Face. Then it travels below the Great Couloir, the Major and the Pear to the Eckpfeiler Buttress where it meets a very steep couloir shooting up to the Col de Peuterey. This journey to the col is six hours of nervous tension, extending through the night. After dawn the whole route is a potential death trap from avalanches and falling stones.

Bonatti's party just made it. With some fifteen metres still to go, the first rays of the sun touched the Col de Peuterey and within minutes an avalanche crashed away from just below them. But they reached the col safely. The Central Pillar of Frêney seemed so near they could almost touch it.

Whilst Bonatti searched for some equipment he and Oggioni had left behind on their last visit the Frenchmen went ahead with the climb, leaving all the pitons in place so that the Italians could climb quickly and catch them up. That night the combined groups had already got higher than Bonatti and Oggioni had done previously. They bivouacked in perfect weather, and next day, to the accompaniment of a spectacularly fiery dawn, continued on their way without much problem. By noon they had reached the foot of the final pinnacle, a seventy-six-metre overhanging monolith known as the Chandelle. It was all that remained between them and victory.

Then, with the dramatic swiftness so common on this side of Mont Blanc, a storm gathered as if from nowhere. Thunder boomed and lightning flickered round the spires; it began to snow and the snow was whipped up by the wind and flung in the faces of the climbers, blinding them. All they could do was gather on such ledges as there were – the Italians together, the French in two groups – and try to sit it out.

They soon discovered that the Pillar had an extra danger. Poking up as it did into the heart of the storm it acted as a natural lightning conductor. Kohlmann was blinded by a flash which grazed his face and, but for prompt action by Mazeaud who sprang up and grabbed him, he would have fallen. The shock of it left Kohlmann temporarily paralysed. As the storm continued unabated, surge after surge of high-voltage electricity passed down the Pillar.

That evening the storm died down to a gentle snowfall. The climbers, numb with shock and mental fatigue, could not rouse themselves enough to cook a meal but simply sat out the freezing hours till dawn. The French, without a bivvy tent, were suffering abominably.

Dawn of the third day was cold and bright, revealing deep cushions of new snow everywhere. A council of war was held and Bonatti gave his opinion that retreat would be extremely difficult and that the best chance of success lay in climbing the Pillar and then making for the Vallot Hut. Given good weather this should not take more than twelve hours, especially as Mazeaud suggested he and Bonatti, as the two strongest, should do the climb and fix ropes to help their companions get up quickly after them. But the break in the weather never came; snow began to swirl round them again. They managed to eat some ham, beef and jam, but were quite unable to boil water for a hot drink.

Wednesday night passed, but Thursday brought no relief and so at dawn on Friday, Bonatti gave orders for a retreat. It had been snowing without respite for sixty hours.

The prospect before them was daunting in the extreme. They had to descend the Frêney Pillar, now iced up, then the Rochers Gruber to the lower Frêney Glacier. From there they had to climb up to the Col de l'Innominata to reach the Gamba Hut on the broad ridge between the Frêney and Brouillard Glaciers. It was a very long line of retreat across difficult terrain, but it was the only way. In the circumstances the Col Eccles and Col de Peuterey – the other ways of escape – were far too dangerous.

So they began twelve hours of continuous abseiling in the teeth of the storm. Bonatti led the way, fixing the ropes, preparing the abseils, then came Mazeaud in a strong position to help the leader or anyone behind who was faltering, then the rest with the faithful Oggioni as last man, recovering the ropes. As Bonatti spiralled down into the swirling snowflakes he had very little idea of where he was or where he was going. On one occasion he found himself isolated in the middle of the vast face, alone in the storm, the rope swung away out of sight. His companions could have abseiled right past him without realising he was there, but Mazeaud's vast experience came to the rescue.

At last they reached the foot of the rocks. The snow was up to their armpits; the cold bitter. They spent the night in a crevasse, moaning and shivering whilst overhead the storm raged in continuing fury. Kohlmann was showing signs of exhaustion and Bonatti noted with concern that the Frenchman also seemed a little light-headed. Guillaume, by a supreme effort of will, managed to brew some tea which helped the sick man revive a little. They ate what remained of the provisions: prunes, chocolate, sugar and a little meat. It was their fifth night in the open.

Next day they continued their descent towards the Rochers Gruber, staggering like drunken men through a sea of shoulder-deep freezing flour. There was no doubt that they all now looked to Bonatti to save them; Bonatti the legendary survivor; the man who always came back. He felt the weight of such responsibility for he knew their chances were slim, though he was heartened by the fact that everyone seemed to have survived the bitter night remarkably well.

But on the slopes above the Rochers Gruber, Antoine Vieille collapsed and died. Only a few months earlier he and Guillaume had made the first winter ascent of the Bonatti Pillar on the Dru. Now the others wrapped his body in the tent to prevent the crows from getting at it and then tied him to a piton.

In a mood of black despair the six survivors began the abseil descent of the Rochers Gruber to the lower Frêney Glacier. Suddenly, through the mist they heard voices calling – rescuers. They shouted back but got no sensible response. Nevertheless, Bonatti and his companions were much heartened by this and when they reached the foot of the rocks at about 3.30, they expected to be greeted with warm food and expert attention. But it was not to be. By a cruel irony the storm lifted momentarily, revealing a completely barren glacier. There were no joyously waving figures, no tracks through the snow even. The voices had been hallucinatory; a common enough phenomenon of mountain stress.

But at least the brief lull in the storm did have its good side – it allowed them to set a proper course for the Gamba Hut. Still wading through snow well above chest height they ploughed furrows towards the Col de l'Innominata, each man choosing his own path, stumbling like automatons. Though they were still roped together, no one cared about safety any more, their own, or anyone else's. It was here that Robert Guillaume collapsed and died.

Meanwhile Bonatti and Gallieni, the two strongest survivors, cast themselves free of the others and forged ahead to try and make the way easy up to the Col de l'Innominata. At the foot of the col they all roped together again for one last desperate effort. Once over the col, the way to the hut and safety would be easy. There was an hour of daylight left.

It was nine o'clock and pitch dark when Bonatti reached the col. The last few feet had been difficult climbing and now, at the top, he could find nowhere for a piton to anchor his companions. All he could do was stand with the rope over his shoulders – at that time the usual way of handling a rope to bring up a companion – and hope that nobody slipped and pulled him off. The wind rose again and whipped the snow into a stinging fury. In the distance thunder and lightning heralded another storm on its way. For three hours Bonatti held the rope, whilst down below his comrades tried to help Andrea Oggioni up the couloir. But Oggioni was far gone. He could not grasp the icy rocks; could not make the one last effort needed to save his life.

Bonatti decided that there was nothing for it except to leave Oggioni and Kohlmann in charge of Mazeaud, who was bearing up well, and with the equally strong Gallieni try to make a rapid push for the Gamba Hut where he knew rescue parties would be assembling. Gallieni came up the gully to join him. Suddenly there was a wild flurry and Kohlmann, perhaps thinking he was being abandoned, came stumbling up the couloir, unroped and climbing like a madman. 'Where's the Gamba Hut?' he croaked, pushing past Gallieni. His eyes were wild and Bonatti recognised madness. Still, they could not abandon him – Gallieni managed to catch hold of him and tie him on the rope between himself and Bonatti.

There was still a lot of dangerous ground to cover – over the crest of the Col de l'Innominata, down the steepish slopes on the other side and then across thankfully easy ground to the hut. The descent became increasingly nightmarish as Kohlmann's dementia grew worse. He flung himself around, threatening to pull them all off the steep slope, shouted and raved and – once they were down – attacked Gallieni, whom he suspected of having a gun and wanting to shoot him! A general mêlée ensued and the two Italians only managed to control Kohlmann by pulling the two ends of the rope in opposite directions and thus isolating him.

It had taken them three hours to descend from the col when it should have taken one. Kohlmann was now beyond all reason, yet the two Italians were tied to him by a rope which was intractable; the knots were frozen solid. They had no knife and they had to keep an eye on Kohlmann who seemed ready to spring at them given the slightest opportunity. Like a spider with its web, Kohlmann relied on the tautness of the rope to warn him of any action by the others. Eventually Bonatti and Gallieni hit on an idea. Keeping the rope taut by holding it in their teeth, they managed to lower their bulky, ice encrusted breeches, and thus slip the rope off round their legs. 'Run!' shouted Bonatti when they were both free.

They were only 400 metres from the hut. They staggered in at three am on the Sunday morning, to find the hut full of sleeping rescuers, who greeted them as though they had returned from the dead. The rescuers found poor Kohlmann in the last stages of his madness and he died in their arms. Oggioni, too, was dead, his lifeless body hanging from a piton in the final couloir. But Mazeaud survived: three men had returned from the seven who set out. Never since the Eigerwand tragedy of 1936 had there been such a disastrous attempt on an Alpine climb.

Despite the horror of Bonatti's ill-fated attempt, others were willing to take up the challenge of the Central Pillar. Scarcely a fortnight after the tragedy, Pierre Julien, an instructor at the École National (the French school of mountaineering), and an Italian climber called Ignazio Piussi were flown to the top of Mont Blanc by helicopter, descended the Peuterey Ridge and cut across the upper Frêney Glacier to the pillar. There was still a lot of snow clinging to the rocks but they managed to climb two-thirds of the pillar before bivouacking for the night. Next day they bivouacked at the foot of the final steep section, the Chandelle. The weather now began to look stormy, but the two men decided to push on. Unfortunately, no sooner had they started on the Chandelle than Piussi dropped the sack containing all their pitons and karabiners. There was nothing for it but to retreat to the Gamba Hut, chased by scudding cloud and snow showers.

In the middle of August a pair of British climbers turned up in Chamonix, intent on climbing the pillar. One was Chris Bonington, the ex-army officer who was destined to become one of the greatest Himalayan experts and a fine rock climber; the other was the short, aggressive little Lancastrian, Don Whillans, one of the best climbers Britain has ever produced. With them came a Pole, Jan Djuglosz, whom they had met at the foot of the Eiger and who was a very fine alpinist. They needed a fourth man to make up two teams of two, which is quicker and more convenient than a rope of three and Djuglosz suggested they ask Julien. At the École, however, Julien excused himself, saying he had other matters to attend to, and it was by chance that Bonington and his companions came across a skilful Yorkshire climber called Ian Clough, whom they knew by repute.

On the afternoon of August 26 the four set out for the Fourche Hut. They took the quickest way, which is via the Midi cable car, but judge their surprise when three heavily laden French climbers also clambered into the car – one of whom was Pierre Julien! The other two were also leading guides: Yves Pollet-Villard and René Desmaison. It didn't take the English long to put two and two together. Julien, alarmed that a strong English party was about to 'steal' the Pillar, had rapidly assembled an equally strong team. However, he too was short of one man and he had cabled his former companion Piussi to meet him at the Torino Hut. Unfortunately, Piussi lived near Trieste, across the width of Italy from Courmayeur, so although he came at once, driving at great speed in a car specially hired for the occasion, there was an inevitable delay. In a race which was none of their making the English climbers had gained an advantage at the outset. They were a day ahead.

Early next morning Bonington's team were on the Col de Peuterey, having marched through the night below the Brenva Face. As they waited for the pillar to be warmed by the rising sun they glanced over into the couloir they had just climbed, expecting to see the French party appear at any moment, not knowing about Piussi. Much to their surprise, a pair of climbers did appear in the couloir, but it was not the French; it was John Harlin and Gary Hemming, two outstanding American climbers. They were having a frightful time in the couloir, now the sun was on the mountain. Incredibly, behind the two Americans, and even more in the line of bombardment, came two of the French, Desmaison and Pollet-Villard, who had left Julien at the Torino Hut to await the tardy Piussi. It was two o'clock in the afternoon before the French finally breasted the Col de Peuterey. They had come through unscathed, though one of the Americans had suffered a slight head wound, which put an end to their hopes of attempting the pillar, and no doubt Harlin thought the outcome was certain, with Whillans and Bonington already well established on the route. The French made no such assumptions and stayed on. Continental climbers of that period were extremely insular in outlook: most of them still believed a myth which had grown since the war that only the Alpine countries produced expert alpinists – the culture shock administered by British, American and Japanese climbers was only just beginning.

Meanwhile the three English and one Pole were romping up the lower sections of the pillar and shortly after three pm they reached the top of a pedestal which was the site of Bonatti's fateful highest bivouac a few weeks earlier. Above them soared the Chandelle.

Whillans, never a one to hang about when there was work to be done, proposed a recce of the next pitch whilst there was still light. Bonington described the action: 'Don, cloth cap planted firmly on his head, a cigarette gripped between his teeth, moved up, slowly and easily. He never seems to hurry when he climbs. Every move, every action is carefully planned – a piton hammered in here, an étrier clipped in, a pause, then a move. The rope never jams.' When the recce ended, both men knew that the way ahead was going to be difficult. Clough and Djuglosz accepted the news stoically and the party set about preparing their bivouac.

Next morning Whillans began his assault on the Chandelle. First of all Bonington climbed up to the high point of the previous evening's exploration, then Whillans pushed the route out from there across a difficult rock bulge and up a corner crack to a jutting roof which he surmounted. When Bonington's

Above: The Frêney Face of Mont Blanc. On right is Col Peuterey and Peuterey Ridge to the summit of Mont Blanc de Courmayeur. The Pillars are clearly shown centre, with the Innominata Ridge to their left. Left again are the Pillars of Brouillard. The Upper Frêney Glacier lies below the Frêney Face with the Rochers Gruber on the right.

Right: Pierre Mazeaud, distinguished French mountaineer and a survivor of the retreat from the Central Pillar in 1961 when four companions died.

The Pillars of Frêney, showing the route up the Central Pillar climbed by Whillans, Bonington, Clough and Duglosz in 1961.
Inset left: Don Whillans, *right:* Chris Bonington.

turn came to follow he found 'everything sloped the wrong way. There were no holds . . . It was a truly remarkable lead by Don.'

Meanwhile, the French had not been idle. Determined to catch up with their rivals, they had cunningly by-passed the lower part of the pillar by means of an easy gully and now emerged at the bivouac place below the Chandelle. Everyone watched as Whillans struggled with a difficult crack, thirty-six metres above their heads.

Suddenly, with a warning cry, Whillans came off. He plunged for fourteen metres before Bonington held him on the rope. As he swung there he let out a plaintive cry, 'I've lost me bloody hat!' Then came grim realisation, 'Me fags were in the hat!' And not only cigarettes, for Whillans was acting as the party's banker and all their worldly wealth was tucked into his hat. Desmaison recalls the surprise he felt at being showered with banknotes.

Bonington now took over the lead but a quick investigation told him that he did not have the right sort of pitons or wedges for the crack which faced him. The French declined to lend him any, saying that they intended to try another line and would need them all – which in fact they did, without success. Meanwhile, Bonington had resorted to a trick invented by British climbers in the 1920s, when pitons were frowned upon in Britain. He dropped into the crack some small stones, choosing those which would jam effectively, and with their aid managed to fix a wedge in the crack and move up nervously on étriers.

He now found himself in the most sensational of exposed positions: 'I have never had such a sense of exposure. There were no holds below my feet. I was jammed across the crack, the walls sloping slightly outwards, rock above me, and either side of me, nothing below, until the couloir dropped steeply a thousand feet lower down.'

He had scarcely strength enough left to reach round to a good hold on the wall and with its aid, pull himself onto a ledge. Then he let out a yell of triumph – the main difficulties were overcome.

Whillans soon joined him but it was too late for Clough and Djuglosz to climb the difficult pitch before dark, so the leader dropped a rope for them to prussik up. The Pole also brought up the end of a French rope, so that Desmaison and his companions could follow next day – the French having finally conceded that the race was lost.

It was all over. The last great problem had been solved.

The last great problem? Every decade has its own last great problem in the mountains and this is perhaps truer of Mont Blanc than anywhere else in the Alps. But the truth is that after the Central Pillar of Frêney there was little that was in the direct line of challenges stretching back 200 years to Paccard and Balmat. There were hard new ascents, like the Walker Direct, but these lacked the grand design; they were technological climbs for a technological age. A vogue for winter climbing grew, and René Desmaison salvaged some Gallic pride by returning to make the first winter ascent of the Central Pillar. With Robert Flematti in the January of 1968 he also solved the long-standing problem of the Shroud – that deadly wall of ice which drapes the Grandes Jorasses to the left of the Walker Spur. Another last great problem . . .

And, of course, in the beginning it all seemed so simple. There was just one problem – to climb Mont Blanc. Little did Paccard and Balmat know what they were starting 200 years ago.

Bibliography

The bibliography of Mont Blanc is considerable, even in English, and the following does not pretend to be comprehensive. English language editions are given for foreign books where possible. The books are listed under the chapters to which they are most appropriate, but some of course spill over into other chapters. Books of a more general nature are listed first. The following abbreviations are used: *AJ=Alpine Journal, AAJ=American Alpine Journal, PPG=Peaks, Passes and Glaciers.*

General

Guide Vallot, Vols I–IV, various authors, Paris, 1975–9
Ball, J., *The Western Alps*, London, 1898
Collomb, R. G., *Mountains of the Alps*, Reading, 1971
Coolidge, W. A. B., *The Alps in Nature & History*, London, 1908
Engel, C. E., *Mont Blanc – an Anthology*, London, 1965
Engel, C. E., *Mountaineering in the Alps*, London, 1971
Frison-Roche, R., *Mont Blanc & the Seven Valleys*, London, 1961
Hiebeler, T., *Lexicon der Alpen*, Gütersloh, 1977
Keenlyside, F., *Peaks and Pioneers*, London, 1975
Milner, C. D., *Mont Blanc & the Aiguilles*, London, 1955
Mumm, A. L., *The Alpine Club Register* (3 vols), London, 1923–8
Neate, W. R., *Mountaineering and its Literature*, Milnthorpe, 1978
Rébuffat, G., *The Mont Blanc Massif*, London, 1975
Unsworth, W., *Encyclopedia of Mountaineering*, London, 1977
Williams, C., *Women on the Rope*, London, 1973
Whymper, E., *Chamonix & the Range of Mont Blanc*, London, 1896

Chapter One

de Beer, G. R., & Brown, T. G., *The First Ascent of Mont Blanc*, London, 1957
Blaikie, T., *Diary of a Scotch Gardener*, London, 1931
Bourrit, M. T., *A Relation of a Journey to the Glaciers in the Duchy of Savoy*, Norwich, 1775
Bourrit, M. T., *Nouvelle description des Glacières de Savoye*, Geneva, 1786
Bourrit, M. T., *Lettre sur le premier voyage au sommet du Mont Blanc*, Geneva, 1786
Dübi, H., *Paccard wider Balmat*, Zurich, 1913

Dumas, A., *Impressions de voyage en Suisse*, Paris, 1832
Freshfield, D. W., *Paccard v Balmat*, *AJ*, 1898
Freshfield, D. W., *The Life of H. B. de Saussure*, London, 1920
Gribble, F., *The Early Mountaineers*, London, 1899
Mathews, C. E., *Annals of Mont Blanc*, London, 1898
Montagnier, H. F., *Dr Paccard's Lost Narrative*, *AJ*, 1911
Montagnier, H. F., *Ascents of Mont Blanc in 1819*, *AJ*, 1920
Montagnier, H. F., *Early History of the Col du Géant*, *AJ*, 1921
Montagnier, H. F., *Thomas Blaikie & Michel-Gabriel Paccard*, *AJ*, 1933
Oxley, T. L., *Jacques Balmat*, London, 1881
de Saussure, H. B., *Voyages dans les Alpes* (4 vols), Neuchâtel, 1779–96
de Saussure, H. B., *Relation abrégée d'un voyage au sommet du Mont Blanc*, Geneva, 1787
Stevens, E. H., *Dr Paccard's Lost Narrative*, *AJ*, 1929

Chapter Two

In the early part of the nineteenth century there were many individual accounts of climbing Mont Blanc. Before Albert Smith came along the best known was probably that by John Auldjo, 1827. A full and detailed bibliography – forty items – by H. F. Montagnier can be found in *AJ* XXV, 1911 and *AJ* XXX, 1916.

Anon, *The Peasants of Chamouni*, London, 1823
Farrar, J. P., *The Brenva Face of Mont Blanc*, *AJ*, 1911
Farrar, J. P., *Days of Long Ago: Charles Hudson*, *AJ*, 1918
Fitzsimmons, R., *The Baron of Piccadilly*, London, 1967
Forbes, J. D., *The Tour of Mont Blanc & Monte Rosa*, London, 1855
Gos, C., *Alpine Tragedy*, London, 1948
Hamel, H., *Reisen auf den Mont Blanc*, Basle, 1820
Hudson, C., & Kennedy, E. S., *Where There's a Will There's a Way*, London, 1856
Moore, A. W., *The Alps in 1864*, London, 1867
Moore, A. W., *Ascent of Mont Blanc from the Glacier de la Brenva*, *AJ*, 1866
Ruskin, J., *The Stones of Venice*, London, 1851
Smith, A., *The Story of Mont Blanc*, London, 1853
Stephen, L., *The Playground of Europe*, London, 1871
Thorington, M., *Mont Blanc Sideshow*, Philadelphia, 1933
Thorington, M., *Albert Smith's Mont Blanc*, *AJ*, 1951/2
Unsworth, W., *Because It Is There*, London, 1968
Wills, A., *The Crossing of the Fenêtre de Saleinaz*, PPG1, 1859
Wills, A., *The Eagle's Nest*, London, 1860
Yeats-Brown, F. A., *Mont Blanc & the Glacier du Miage*, *AJ*, 1869

Chapter Three

Buxton, E. N., *Mont Blanc & the Glacier du Dôme*, *AJ*, 1865
Clark, R. W., *The Early Alpine Guides*, London, 1949

Bibliography

Clark, R. W., *The Day the Rope Broke*, London, 1965
Cunningham, C. D., & Abney, W. de W.,*The Pioneers of the Alps*, London, 1887
Dangar, D., *Christian Almer and Melchior Anderegg*, *AJ*, 1946
George, H. B., *The Col de la Tour Noire*, *AJ*, 1863/4
Reilly, A. M. W. Adams, *Some New Ascents in the Chain of Mont Blanc*, *AJ*, 1865
Smythe, F. A., *Edward Whymper*, London, 1940
Unsworth, W., *Matterhorn Man*, London, 1965
Whymper, E., *Scrambles Amongst the Alps*, London, 1871

Chapter Four

Brown, T. G., *The History of the Innominata Face of Mont Blanc*, *AJ*, 1949
Dent, C. T., *Above the Snow Line*, London, 1885
Eccles, J., *The Brouillard & Fresnay Glaciers*, *AJ*, 1878
Farrar, J. P., *The Aiguille Blanche de Peuterey*, *AJ*, 1920
Girdlestone, A. G., *The High Alps Without Guides*, London, 1870
King, H. S., *First Ascent of the Aiguille Blanche de Peuterey*, *AJ*, 1885
Maund, J. O., *The Aiguille Verte from the Argentière Glacier*, *AJ*, 1877
Middlemore, T., *The Col des Grandes Jorasses*, *AJ*, 1876

Chapter Five

Carr, E., *Two Days on an Ice Slope*, *AJ*, 1893
Collie, J. N., *The Ascent of the Dent du Requin*, *AJ*, 1894
Collie, J. N., *Climbing in the Himalaya etc*, London, 1902
Hastings, G., *Over Mont Blanc by the Brenva Route Without a Guide*, *AJ*, 1895
Kugy, J., *Alpine Pilgrimage*, London, 1934
Mummery, A. F., *My Climbs in the Alps & Caucasus*, London, 1895
Unsworth, W., *Tiger in the Snow*, London, 1967

Chapter Six

Duke of the Abruzzi, *The First Ascent of Punta Jolanda*, *AJ*, 1903
Blodig, K., *Die Viertausender der Alpen*, Munich, 1923
Güssfeldt, P., *Mont Blanc*, Geneva, 1898
Klucker, C., *Adventures of an Alpine Guide*, London, 1932
Mallory, G. L., *Mont Blanc by the East Buttress of Mont Maudit*, *AJ*, 1918
Mallory, G. L., *A New Route Up the Charmoz*, *AJ*, 1919
Purtscheller, L., *Uber Fels und Firn*, Munich, 1901
Rébuffat, G., *Chamonix-Mont Blanc 1900*, Geneva, 1981
Tairraz, G., *The Tairraz Family of Chamonix*, *AJ*, 1975
Young, G. W., *On High Hills*, London, 1927

Chapter Seven

Blanchet, E. R., *Hors des Chemins battus*, Paris, 1932
Charlet, A., *Ma Vocation Alpine*, Neuchâtel, 1950
Courtauld, S. L., *The Innominata Face of Mont Blanc*, AJ, 1949
Damesme, M., & de Lepiney, T., *The Early Years of the GHM*, AJ, 1970
de Lepiney, J. & T., *Climbs on Mont Blanc*, London, 1930
Roch, A., *Climbs of My Youth*, London, 1949
Underhill, M., *Give Me the Hills*, London, 1956

Chapter Eight

Agresti, H., *Winter Climbing in the Mont Blanc Massif*, AJ, 1972
Brown, T. G., *Brenva*, London, 1944
Calvert, H., *Smythe's Mountains*, London, 1985
Cassin, R., *Italian Climbing between the Wars*, AJ, 1972
Gervasutti, G., *Gervasutti's Climbs*, London, 1957
Heckmair, A., *Main German and Austrian Climbers since 1930*, AJ, 1969
Heckmair, A., *My Life as a Mountaineer*, London, 1975
Roberts, E., *Welzenbach's Climbs*, Reading, 1980
Scott, D., *Big Wall Climbing*, London, 1974
Smythe, F. S., *Climbs & Ski Runs*, London, 1929
Smythe, N., *Francis Sydney Smythe: mountain photographer*, AJ, 1976

Chapter Nine

Cassin, R., *50 Years of Alpinism*, London, 1981
Frendo, E., *La Face Nord des Grandes Jorasses*, Lausanne, 1947
Magnone, G., *West Face*, London, 1955
Pyatt, E., *The Passage of the Alps*, London, 1984
Roch, A., *Mon Carnet de Courses*, Lausanne, 1948
Sharp, P., *Tunnels through the Alps*, AJ, 1979

Chapter Ten

Bonatti, W., *On The Heights*, London, 1964
Bonington, C., *I Chose To Climb*, London, 1966
Brown, J., *The Hard Years*, London, 1967
Chrobak, E., *New Route on the Grand Pilier d'Angle*, AJ, 1970
Chrobak, E., *Pointe Hélène*, AJ, 1972
Clough, I., *A Season of Plenty*, AJ, 1962
Desmaison, R., *Total Alpinism*, London, 1982
Harlin, J., *First Ascents in the Mont Blanc Alps*, AAJ, 1964
Harlin, J., *The North Face of the Petit Dru Direct*, AJ, 1966
Mazeaud, P., *Naked Before The Mountain*, London, 1974
Ullman, J. R., *Straight Up*, New York, 1968
Whillans, D., & Ormerod, A., *Don Whillans: Portrait of a Mountaineer*, London, 1971.

Index